Praise for
I Want To Be Me But I Don't Know Who I Am

We're all aware that the adolescent social/emotional landscape is treacherous and filled with internal and external challenges. The central question is "how can we help teens navigate it successfully?" Dr. B to the rescue! This book gives teens all they need to succeed in today's world. Everything from goal-setting to problem-solving is covered in a manner that connects warmly with high-school aged kids; the Identity and Behavior Scales are particularly helpful. Highly recommended!

--*John H. Morris, LMSW-ACP, LMFT*

I like this book and wish I had it for my own teens when they were growing up. The writing style is warm and comfortable. The author will seem like an older (and wiser) friend after a few pages. I'd say—read, enjoy, share with your friends and talk about it. What do they think?

--*Allen E. Ivey, Ed.D., ABPP*
Distinguished University Professor (Emeritus),
University of Massachusetts, Amherst

Dr. Boskovitz has written an engaging book for teens who will enjoy the conversational tone and no-pressure approach. The examples are easy to relate to and the format will pull the reader forward. The scales and decision tree exercises engage the reader with the material.

--*Harriet Arvey, Ed.D., Consultant*
Communities in Schools of Houston.
Formerly - Assistant Superintendent, Houston
Independent School District.

Dr. Boskovitz taps into the central goal of adolescence: identity development. Her straight-forward method empowers teens and young adults to discover who they are and what they value. I look forward to sharing this valuable tool with parents and teens.

--Hillery Keith, Ph.D. Adjunct Professor
University of St. Thomas, Houston, TX

I Want To Be Me But I Don't Know Who I Am will be a beacon for teens in this frequently overwhelming stage of their lives. It will be a place where adolescents can get help/guidance to make decisions for their life and find refuge/protection from undue influences. This book's methods will empower teenagers and help them build confidence when confidence can seem elusive.

In deaf education, visuals are extremely important; deaf students will benefit from this book and its problem-solving work sheets.

--Joan Kosinski, B.A., Interpreter for the Deaf,
Pre-K through College
Interpreted for Vice-President Joe Biden

This book is an absolute must for therapists, school counselors, teachers, and parents of teens and young adults. Dr. B. uses a fresh, down to earth approach to engage teens. The book offers them practical tools for gaining insight about themselves and increasing their ability to make positive changes.

--Dr. Susan Chanderbhan, Psychologist

I Want To Be Me
But I Don't Know Who I Am

I Want To Be Me
But I Don't Know Who I Am

◆ ◆ ◆

A Guidebook for Teens and Young Adults

Madeleine Boskovitz, Ph.D.

CorymarC Publishing

<u>Author's Note to the Reader:</u> This book is meant to offer advice and encourage-
ment to teens and young adults. It does not offer or replace professional psychological or therapeutic treatment, nor is it meant to replace other professional
interventions.

ISBN: 0998778605
ISBN 13: 9780998778600
Library of Congress Control Number: 2017903316
CorymarC Publishing, Houston,TEXAS
Published in the United States by CorymarC Publishing, Houston, Texas

Publisher's Cataloging-In-Publication Data
(Prepared by The Donohue Group, Inc.)

Names: Boskovitz, Madeleine.
Title: I want to be me but I don't know who I am : a guidebook for teens and
young adults / Madeleine Boskovitz, Ph.D.
Description: Houston, Texas : CorymarC Publishing, [2017] | Series: I want to be
me ; [volume 1] | Interest age level: 013-020.
Identifiers: LCCN 2017903316 | ISBN 0-9987786-0-5 | ISBN 978-0-9987786-0-0
| ISBN 978-0-9987786-1-7 (ebook)
Subjects: LCSH: Self-actualization (Psychology) in adolescence--Handbooks,
manuals, etc. | Self-esteem in adolescence--Handbooks, manuals, etc. | Self-
esteem in young adults--Handbooks, manuals, etc. | Self-confidence in adoles-
cence--Handbooks, manuals, etc. | Resilience (Personality trait) in adolescence-
-Handbooks, manuals, etc. | Self-help techniques for teenagers--Handbooks,
manuals, etc. | Adolescent psychology--Handbooks, manuals, etc. | Teenagers-
-Conduct of life--Handbooks, manuals, etc. | Young adults--Conduct of life-
-Handbooks, manuals, etc.
Classification: LCC BF724.3.S25 B67 2017 (print) | LCC BF724.3.S25 (ebook) |
DDC 155.5--dc23

Dr. Boskovitz gratefully acknowledges Catherine Dolto, M.D., for permission
to translate and adapt a brief excerpt from Françoise Dolto, M.D. and Catherine
Dolto, M.D.: Paroles pour les adolescents ou le complexe du homard, Gallimard,
2003.
Dr. Boskovitz thanks Terri St. Cloud at https://www.bonesigharts.com for
permission to reprint her poem: a tree's whisper.
Cover Font: © Paratype
Cover Photos and Cameos: © Adobe Stock Photos
Cover design: RC Creative, Marc Sawaya ©2017

This book is dedicated to teens and young adults
– for they are the future

"...you are in the age of adolescence...you who feel that what you are living is difficult. People talk about adolescence...but it is seldom that they talk to you about those difficulties..."

--Adapted from Françoise Dolto, M.D. & Catherine Dolto, M.D. Paroles pour adolescents ou le complexe du homard. Gallimard. 2003

Foreword

Nine Steps to Better Awareness

Teens and young adults yearn to know themselves and learn how to lead their lives. They need to become empowered to develop their best selves. In this book,

- You'll discover where you are now with the Identity and Behavior Scales.
- You'll also know where you want to be: know your needs.
- You'll see your dreams more clearly
- You'll find your path to your goals
- You'll feel your strength and your power to meet your goals
- You'll avoid the pitfalls and the distractions that keep you from meeting your goals
- You'll learn how to make small and big decisions with confidence and self-knowledge
- You'll become able to seek the help you need along the way.
- You'll become empowered to be you even in the face of large obstacles or problems

Table of Contents

Note: The Behavior and Identity Scales and a blank Decision Tree are available for download at www.iwanttobeme.org. Please use Code: <u>bisdt2017</u>.

Introduction

My Promise to You

In this book, I am going to be talking about the teen and young adult experience. You will note that you already know a lot of things. Just like we teach toddlers to recognize and name their body parts -- parts they already know, since they are part of them -- I will help you identify the various parts of you and your life. I have found that young people really like to see themselves from the outside. This book will teach you awareness of who you are and what choices you make. It will also teach you how to make decisions that work for you.

<u>**A most important concept or idea: Awareness**</u>: this is the most important concept, because it gives you freedom. So, naming your qualities and behaviors will help you be more aware of yourself, of who you are, what you do, and how others see you. You will come to understand the freedom and the responsibility that you have. Once you understand your personality and your behavior, and the choices you make, you will be more able to make choices that serve your desires and goals.

The teen years are a very important time: you are laying the foundations for your adult life. All the good things you do for yourself now will pay you back more than ten-fold later. On the other hand, any serious mistakes that you make now can come back to haunt you during your adult life. Yet, this is the best time to be making mistakes and to be learning from them. Most teens make mistakes that are the usual mistakes that we make in those years. We make poor decisions about little things and consequences are small and manageable. Sometimes, we make poor decisions about bigger things. Those are the ones that we may have to live with for a long time, sometimes our whole lives. Some mistakes affect our health and others limit our later choices, such as becoming a parent very early in life.

Sometimes, teens' mistakes get them involved in the legal system but even these mistakes are often manageable. Teens are usually considered minors and their juvenile records are sealed when they reach adult age, so that their mistakes don't get in their way later. In some cases, however, for very serious crimes, this may not be true. For young adults, getting involved with the law is even more harmful; it is likely to haunt them for the rest of their lives.

So, what help can I be, I who am very interested in helping teens and young adults? I can help you be more aware of choosing because, of course, you make choices all the time. Being able to make choices that work for you makes all the difference: learning how to think about what we are choosing makes the difference.

<u>Another most important concept: Identity</u>. Identity is how you see and describe yourself, and how others see you. An easy way is to think of naming the easy facts about yourself: gender (if you like, include sexual orientation), eye color, hair color, age, height, weight, name, parents' names, number of brothers and sisters, school grade, school average, courses you are taking. This list goes on and on. There are a lot of facts about who you are. You can probably think of more that are important to you.

But there are less obvious facts about everyone, as well. These are the facts about your inner self and private behaviors. What are your qualities? How do you act? Other people see those as well, even though you may think they are invisible to others. To help you measure those, I have created the Identity Scale and the Behavior Scale. (These are online and at the back of this book, in the appendix).

The Identity Scale. Many years ago, I created this scale which lets you rate your own personality traits for my work with young teens in a shelter. They entirely understood it and seemed to like it very much. It gave them a picture of the person they were now, who they had been before their teen years, and who they wanted to become. It gave them an awareness of how they felt about their life and themselves. In Chapter 1, you will learn how to use the Identity Scale to think about yourself. It will also help you see how you change over time.

The Behavior Scale. This one came along much later, while writing this book, as a matter of fact. I came to think that labeling and being aware of your behaviors is as important as knowing your traits. There, too, you could look at your behaviors in the past, where you stand now, and where you want to go. I think you will find measuring your changes on this scale also very exciting and helpful.

Decision Trees. These will help you learn how to think about decisions and how to make decisions that you like. We all make decisions all the time, but we often don't think about making decisions. It seems to just sort of happen. But we make decisions all the time--and it is very important to think about them—we make little decisions and much bigger ones as well. Decision trees will help you look into the future and see the outcome and consequences of your decisions. You can make decisions that fit you really well when you use the decision trees.

Here are the nine steps that I promised you. They will help you figure out what you need to make your life the way you want. I will explain each step, in detail, in the following chapters and you will have the blank Decision Tree, and the Identity and Behavior charts to use. These charts are your private space to work things out for yourself.

1. As you use the Identity and the Behavior Scales, you'll discover where you have been, where you are now and where you want to be. You will make the scales yours. You can use the components that are already there and you can add your own components, ones that only you know you need. You'll be able to figure out which personality strengths are already yours and which ones you want to develop, which behaviors work for you and which ones you want to change. (Please make copies of the scales that are at the back of this book or download them from the www.iwanttobeme.org website for your own use).

2. You'll figure out where you want to be; you'll know what your goals are. When you see what you want your life to look like, you can see your goals. The chapters in this book will help you find ways to get to your goals.

3. You'll be able to see the path to your dreams much more clearly. Life is lived one day at a time but every step can take you nearer to your goal or it can move you away from your goal. Keeping your goal in mind is the most important.

4. You'll be able to plan your path to your goals. It is most important to be able to tell which steps are in the right direction and which are not. It will help you to avoid going the wrong way.

5. You'll find your strengths and your power to meet your goals. You will probably be surprised at your strengths and your power. It's so easy to feel confused or even discouraged, but when you know which steps to take, you feel your dreams are much more reachable.

6. You'll avoid the pitfalls and the distractions that keep you from meeting your goals. This is most important, as there are always temptations and challenges. This book will help you find ways to avoid or overcome them. It will even help you get back on the path if you've been going in the wrong direction. It's never too late.

7. You'll learn how to make big decisions with confidence and self-knowledge. Most of life is about little everyday decisions, but we are all also faced with big decisions. Decision Trees will be explained; they are very useful tools for learning how to make decisions, big and small. Of course, you'll do that privately as well.

8. You'll find the help you need along the way. "No man is an island," said the great poet, John Donne. We all need help all the time and it is important to know how and where to get it.

It's important to know whom you can count on or not. This book will help you here, too.

9. You'll become empowered to be you, even in the face of large obstacles or problems. These steps are for you to take now during your teen and young adult years to get ready for your adult life; they are something that you will use all the time in your future life.

My promise is that if you read this book and work with the Scales and the Decision Trees, you'll come to trust your decisions and feel more confident and satisfied with your life now. In addition, you will have more motivation to think your dreams possible and make greater efforts to reach them.

Chapter 1

Calling Dr. B

Who am I and why would I want to talk to teens and young adults?

So, let me start with the "who I am."

I am a psychologist. I have always been fascinated by people; I have wanted to understand why people are the way they are. How do children become the adults they turn into? Even more important, how do they turn into the persons they want to become?

I have discovered that this is a question that is very important to teens and even young adults. They are the ones who are turning into something. That something is adults. But teens don't know what adults they will turn into. They are often confused and even scared of that independence and responsibility, if they'll admit it.

In my work with teens in schools, in shelters, in neighborhood programs, and even in my office where they come for help when they feel stuck or in too much conflict with their parents, I have found that most young people love to talk and to hear about themselves as they struggle to understand their life. In my office, I see many young adults who are also struggling with knowing who they are and what they want. This is totally normal and healthy and not true of only teens and young adults: most people want to know what makes them the persons they are. Most people struggle with their choices and their decisions and want to have more satisfying lives.

There is so much going on around us that it is often confusing. How do we know what we really want? How do we get it, once we know? How do we make a plan? How do we stay on track? How do we get back on track when we get lost?

All these are very important questions for teens, young adults, and everyone else. I think teens are even more in need of explanations, as this is their first time trying to understand their world and how to be in it. I feel teens are often eager to know what needs to happen for them to be ready for the adult world.

One teen said to me recently: "I want to be me but I don't know who I am." That said it all! She was trying to be true to herself but she felt confused, unsure of what she needed. The world is a very complicated place for all of us, but it is particularly complicated for teens.

But don't be discouraged. Adolescence – the teen and young adult years– can be very exciting. You are at the beginning of your independent life. This is the time you are struggling to find out who you are AND who you want to become. But don't be afraid, you have plenty of time. Many young people feel too much pressure to get there, but you have more than ten years, starting with the pre-teen years, to become an adult! That's a very long time! Yes, there is a lot to learn but take it easy. Life is lived from day to day. There is time.

But know also that what good you do for yourself now will serve you many times over when you are an adult. Whatever harm you bring to yourself will also come back to you many times later. You are building the foundation of your life. So, build carefully and slowly. Take your time. There is no rush. Lay that foundation one solid brick at a time.

 Examples of good bricks are studying for a test or practicing your favorite baseball skills because you want to get on the team. You are acquiring knowledge, testing your knowledge, building your skills, contributing to your grade point average, or your future chances at a sports scholarship (maybe you want to go to college). An example of a brick that will harm you later is posting a picture of yourself on the internet that shows you in an unfavorable light, such as showing inappropriate postures or body parts. It may be funny now, but it won't be so funny when a college admission reviewer sees it and denies you admission to your favorite college (things never disappear from the internet —not even Snapchat -- and they are quite easy to find).

Very soon in this chapter, you will read and learn how to consider decisions that you make all the time and how to consider their consequences. My Decision Trees will guide you in learning how to think through the possible consequences of the choices you make.

Many books are written for parents to help them understand and help their teens. Most of them are wonderful but the teens don't read them. They get the help that their parents can give them. Sometimes their parents do provide the help and coaching they need, but many parents are too busy to read those books and they are not always available to help their children the way that is needed.

But you're the expert on what you're feeling and thinking. **I think that speaking directly to you is a better option.** You can think about yourself and know your needs; you can use the tools in this book to help you find your answers. This book will give you tools to find out who you are and who you want to be.

So, how do you become the person you want to be? How do you grow from the dependence of a child to the independence of an adult? It is quite an assignment. But remember that you have time. The answers come when you take your time and learn how to make choices that fit you. Learn to hear your inner voice – it will tell you what is right or wrong for yourself.

<u>Your inner voice</u>. We all have a voice in our head (no, we're not crazy) that keeps track of everything we do. This is a great gift that human beings have. We can think about who we are and what we do. As we grow up, we become more aware of ourselves and what we think, feel, and do. We tend to look at our emotions, thoughts and

behavior and think about them. We have feelings and even exercise judgment toward our feelings, thoughts, and behavior.

Some people call it a conscience. Others call it a guiding voice. I like to call it our inner voice because it is a very important part of each of us. Where does it come from? Mostly, it comes from what we have learned about the world and about ourselves from our parents. Hopefully, that voice is positive, encouraging, loving. It tells us firmly what is right and wrong. It tells us what we should or should not do. It rewards us when we are good and gently punishes us when we make mistakes. We feel good about ourselves when we act with the voice and often feel regret or guilt when we act against our inner voice. During the teen and young adult years, this voice becomes less that of our parents and more our own voice, as we choose what we want to keep and what we want to discard.

Unfortunately, sometimes, the voice that we inherit from our parents is difficult to live with. It is discouraging, rather than encouraging. We have learned that we are not "good," or that we are "a failure, that we'll never amount to much," that whatever we want to do, we won't be able to. This is an abusive voice and it must be silenced in our head. We must kick it out and find again our own voice that tells us that we're alright, that we can succeed, that we are worthwhile persons.

Sometimes, we're in so much pain from the bad voices we hear that our inner voice is very loud, telling us to get away from the pain. Here, we have to be very careful to listen to the good voice that will guide us on the right path. Too often, the pain is so much that we just want to shut it out with drugs or escape in computer games. But that won't help us. We need to find our inner voice that will talk to us of our goodness and hope, and give us the strength to move forward. There is help in the schools and in the community. In later chapters, I will encourage you to seek help as needed.

So, how do we retrieve our own good voice? Sometimes, I have helped teens and even youngsters become their own caring parent, rewarding and guiding themselves in their life. It can be done by kids as young as 7. You can do it if you need to and it is the best gift you can give yourself. You become your own guide in your life. Eventually, we all get to this step of becoming our own guides in our lives. This is what helps us make the best decisions for ourselves.

Trust that this inner voice is there even if it is hard to hear sometimes, even if it must be pulled out from our very core. But it tells us who we are, who we need to become to be happy with ourselves. We call that being true to ourselves, being in harmony with ourselves. That voice helps us grow throughout our lives. It is what keeps us moving forward, tackling obstacles, succeeding, enjoying.

Look at Where You Are:
The Identity Scale & the Behavior Scale

The Scales will help you look in the mirror and become more self-aware. But just as a mirror doesn't lie, the Scales are useful only if you are very honest with yourself. It is private; no one else needs to see it. The Scales will help you understand where you are now, where you have been and, most important, where you want to go. (See the Appendix for information on how to download the scales from the Web).

If you look at the scales, you can choose the qualities and behaviors you want to look at; you can add important ones of your own. What's the purpose? Is keeping track of yourself important? I think it can be very helpful. It can help you appreciate your efforts and their success. It can help you spot your difficulties. It can make you aware of when you are slipping back, falling off the path. It can help you identify what you need to change. Many times, we don't know how we will feel about a choice we make. We can only judge afterwards if it was a good choice or one we are unhappy with. Using the scale helps us understand ourselves and what we can expect to feel.

 Let's try an example: demonstration of the Scales in operation.

Let's say you want to go to a party with some friends Saturday night, but you have a test on Monday morning and you know deep down (that's the little voice) that you are not well prepared for the test. You might even fail if you don't study enough. You're actually close to failing the semester. What to do? You're afraid that if you don't go to the party, you'll be missing out on the fun. Also, others may call you a dork if you stay home to study. On the other hand, you sure don't want to fail the test as you are in danger of failing the class...and that means summer school...

Or maybe you have a sports practice early in the morning. You really want to get on the team and be one of the popular kids. However, you know you are not that good and you really need to practice as much as possible.

This is called a dilemma or situation where the choices you have are really hard and you're not sure what to do. We are faced with this kind of situation all the time. How do we decide? How would the scale help? What are my goals?

Let's say you go to the party and you end up failing the test. You enjoyed the party but now you feel quite nervous about passing the class. Or maybe you know you can't pass. You will be going to summer school.

Or you missed the practice. The coach was irritated with you and told you that you're not likely to make the team if you don't take the practices seriously.

Go to the Scales and see where you are now in terms of happiness, of hopefulness.

Let's say you listened to your inner voice and you stayed home and studied for the test. You could catch up with the gossip about the party with your best friend later. You passed the test and it looks like you will be able to pass the semester.

You got to the practice early the next morning. The coach was very impressed with you. There is a good chance that he will pick you for the team.

Check the scale. Which way have you moved? How does it feel? Are you happier, more hopeful, more ambitious, feeling that maybe you can succeed? You just have to stay focused on your goal.

As you grow more toward adulthood, you will become more aware of choices and their results, their consequences. Maybe, you've been checking out the scales to see how they work. I hope you are looking at them. But if you decided not to, that is your choice. This book is all about making choices and taking responsibility for them. So, if you decide later to come back and check out the scales, I hope you'll find them useful.

This leads right into a glimpse at the next part: learning how to make choices. You have been making choices for a long time. You make decisions all the time...so, what's the big deal? Maybe you are aware that everything you choose has a consequence, big or small. Maybe you're not: you make decisions about things without thinking and are not always pleased with their outcome.

Well, you may want to learn how to make choices so that you are happy with the outcome. Maybe, you can even predict the outcome so that it is easier to choose. Grown-ups seem to know how to make choices. Yes. They have more experience. They also try to look into the future and be aware of consequences. Hopefully, you've been learning that, too.

Decision Trees: decision trees help in looking at what happens, at the consequences of choices. I will show you how they work in the Appendix. It may look difficult at first, but you'll soon get the hang of it and it'll become familiar. Again, you may find it useful or not.

But you'll know it's there if you want to try it out with a tough decision, or even any decision. It is good to get practice with little, everyday decisions, such as having breakfast or skipping it. What to have for breakfast? Go ahead and try it out. You'll see it's not all that hard.

Do this exercise with me to understand and predict consequences. This is important because we can often predict some of what will happen. For example, you know from experience that if you skip breakfast, you are likely to be hungry long before lunch.

What you may not be thinking of is that you'll be in math class at the time when you are really hungry. Math is hard for you (and for many others) and you have already fallen behind. So, if you are hungry, it makes it even harder to pay attention to a tough subject. You might not be paying attention at all. You'll be thinking about other things or your hungry stomach. You'll feel even more lost in class. What happens then? Will you be tempted to think: "I just give up? I am no good at math. What's the use?" That's one branch of the tree. (Look at the decision tree in the Appendix. It shows exactly how this works).

The other is you have breakfast, are focused during math class, and then you actually understand something that you didn't understand the day before. You feel excited, energized. It's not that hard and you can get it. Maybe, you could even be good at it.

You will see from the Decision Tree that there are forks in the road everywhere. So, go back to the previous paragraph. You did not have breakfast and you got distracted and discouraged in your math class. But it's not too late. It is never too late. You can talk to the teacher, go to an after-school tutorial, ask friends for help, ask parents for help. You can even decide to have breakfast the next day so that you can be more comfortable and keep up with classwork.

These decision trees help you think more like adults – which is exactly what you want. You want to crack the code of how to become a grown-up. After all, you will be a young adult at the end of this decade. (A decade is ten years; the second decade goes from 10 to 20 years of age). Remember, I told you that every good brick you lay will pay you back ten-fold…learning how to make decisions is the most important skill you can learn because you have to make decisions about everything every day, for your whole life.

You will also be making big choices: choosing friends, making important decisions such as whether to have sex, whether to use drugs, get drunk, get pregnant, big decisions that can affect your whole life in big ways. We make these big decisions for ourselves, whether we decide ahead of time or just jump into things on a moment's notice. These are still decisions. They do not just happen.

But in these important moments it is most often impossible to really think things through because you can't use a decision tree when you feel under pressure to decide. You will be with friends or a boyfriend or girlfriend, and you will feel pressured to go along. One very good way, the best way, is to have decided ahead of time on these big decisions. You can think about them ahead of time and then it is much easier to remember your decisions when you're under pressure.

Earlier, I talked to you about listening to your inner voice. When you're under pressure to choose in the moment, something which happens to many people, it's most important to listen to the good voice inside of you, the voice that wants you to be true to yourself, the voice that wants you to have the best life you can have – and it can be a good life.

Thus, it is easiest and best for you if you make those big decisions ahead of time, being careful to listen to your voice and to think things through, to consider the consequences. You use the decision trees in your head or on paper. You need the skills and the time to make those big decisions.

You also need to use the decision-making process and listen to your inner voice when it comes to choosing friends. This is most important. You want friends who are good to you and good for you. You want friends that will respect your decisions and not put undue pressure on you to engage in behaviors when you don't want to.

Unfortunately, this happens very often with teens. They find themselves with people they like and who want to tempt them to try things such as drugs, alcohol, or even sex. Every teen is curious about these things. These are the things of the adult world. They are fascinating. Thus, it will be good if you have thought about it before hand and are not making a decision on the fly. But that happens too. Know that you are not different from most teens.

This is what makes decisions so difficult. But choosing to do something once doesn't mean that you have to choose to do it again, if you don't want to. You learn which friends you want in your circle and which not. You can also learn from watching others at school and in the neighborhood. You learn what they are about before you even join up with them.

I hope you will let your inner voice guide you to make the choices that you want to live with, the decisions that fit you and your goals.

Some of you may be thinking to yourselves: "This is never going to help me. My parents are on welfare. I am on welfare. I don't have a future. I probably won't even finish high school." This may be your situation for now but it is still important to have dreams and goals. Without them, it won't get any better for you. But with them, you can learn to make yourself a different future.

Let me tell you the immigrant story. Immigrants are people who come to the United States to make a better life for themselves. They have a vision and a goal. They want change. They know that change takes time. It may well be that it will take a generation, sometimes two, depending on circumstances. They plan for the long run. They do their best to raise their children so they, in turn, will have better opportunities. Maybe the children will go to college and raise themselves out of poverty.

My parents brought us to the States when my sister and I were teenagers. They worked hard to be able to afford us not working while we attended college. My sister and I both went to a free city-college and fulfilled our parents' dream of going further in school than they did. We could make a better life for ourselves.

I was just reading about the life of First Lady Michelle Obama. Her parents were very poor. Her father held a night job at a plant to take care of his family. Her mother stayed home and raised her and her brother. Neither parent had an education. But Michelle could win scholarships to the best Ivy League schools.

It's not necessary to go to the best schools to have a good life. But finishing college definitely lifts you out of poverty. Many more doors are open to you when you have a college degree. When your children succeed, it is your success also. When you succeed, it is your parents' success, too.

So, even if college is not in your future for now, it's still a good goal. There are scholarships and grants for people wanting to go to college later in life. There are just so many options. It is up to you to make them work for you. If your heart and mind are set on making yourself a better life, the chances are very good that you will have a better life.

You may be waiting for me to give you the usual lectures about alcohol, drugs, and sex, but I won't. I am not here to tell you what to do. You see, that's what becoming a grown-up means: you tell yourself what to do. I trust that if you use this book, pay attention to your inner voice that guides you toward life and health, and learn how to make decisions, you will be well able to make those decisions for yourself.

You will not only decide which way you want to go, you will decide when you want to make that decision for yourself. Your parents have rules for you: those are good guidelines. I was strict with my children: I told them that adult things were to be saved for when they were of legal age. As long as they lived at home, they were children and didn't make adult decisions about alcohol, drugs, or sex. I think the rules helped them. They knew my expectations. What they actually did, I don't know. I didn't know then and I still don't know now. I didn't really need to know – those were their decisions.

I hope that you will consider your responsibility to yourself and to your future. You will realize that decisions you make now impact your future life. Some decisions are easy for some people but not for others. Whichever way, decisions get made and you will live with the consequences. Also, it is most important to realize that even if you take a wrong turn, make a poor decision that turns out to harm you, you can always get back on track to taking good care of yourself.

How do I know what you need? I don't. But I can help you figure out what you need and how to get there. I am a psychologist – I study how people grow into the persons they become. I help along the way if it is difficult for them. I have helped many children, teens, young adults, and even older adults when they got confused and lost their path. Becoming one's self, the person we choose to be, is a lifelong project. We are always becoming.

But right now, your job is to go from a dependent child to an independent young adult. That is a very big task for anyone. You have time during that second decade of your life – a whole ten years – and beyond: take your time. Choose carefully what you do. Become the person you want to become.

I want to remind you that I won't lecture you about sex and drugs. Those are very personal decisions. If you use my book, you will find yourself able to make those decisions for yourself. You will understand your choices and know the responsibility you have to yourself.

Chapter 2

Early Skills Lead to Self-Sufficiency

Before we jump into the second decade of life, it is important to see what foundation you have built for yourself in the first ten years. What kind of support will it provide for you in this second decade? It is essential to notice what you have already accomplished. You may not think about it, but it was a lot. When you think that you started life as a helpless newborn and became a nearly independent youngster in ten years, you can see that you have already learned a lot of things.

In the first year, you learned to recognize people and objects around you. Then you learned to name them. This is very important, as I wrote in the first chapter. Once you name, you can act with true purpose. As an infant, you would reach toward an object but be incapable of informing others. You would cry if frustrated. With words, you could communicate your desire, ask for the object. You had already begun to realize that you were separate from others. Now you could begin to communicate and exchange with others.

Also, in the first year, you learned to manage your body: rolling over, sitting, crawling, and walking. This was quite challenging but you had this inner force that drove you to achieve these steps. Babies will keep trying to get up and walk. They will fall and sometimes cry and then try again and again until they are able to do it. Then they move on to the next thing, maybe climbing or running. They just don't stop. They have a world to conquer, to take their place among the others.

Then, in the second year, you learned another hard step, you learned to manage your bodily needs, feeding yourself and becoming able to control your toileting, your bodily functions. This was the first step toward learning the rules of the world and toward being independent. When babies can manage their bodies, they don't need others to do it for them. One more step toward autonomy. Autonomy is ruling ourselves. You also learned to get around in the world of objects as you encountered them at home and outside.

After you turned two, in your third year, you entered the "terrible twos." This is the time when the child has to learn to accept and respect limits – the NO. You had to learn to manage your behavior, to obey the rules imposed by the adults around you. This is a challenging time for children and parents because children also learn that they can say "NO" as well. They then continually test their will against the adult's. They then test the rules at every moment in order to learn them and their limits.

While you learned that you could say NO to others, you were also learning that you are a separate person, that you have choices. When you were two or three-years old, your NO didn't have much power. Maybe saying "NO" even got you in trouble with your parents. Still, it was the very beginning of your independence. This was a very important time. This was when you began to learn how your parents would handle your independence. Did your parents give you enough space, too much, too little? Enough independence allowed you to become comfortable with yourself. Too much independence and the child is out of control, doesn't know how he needs to behave. Not enough independence, then the child is either shy and hesitant or angry, depending on temperament. What they did helped make you the person that you are today.

In middle childhood, from 3 to 6 years of age, you learned the rules of conduct at home, you learned what you were allowed to touch or not, what you could do or not. You also learned the rules of the physical world: how to avoid hot things, you learned about heights and when you could safely jump or not. You began to learn to avoid putting yourself in danger. You stayed close to your parents when out in the community. You held your parents' hand when crossing the street. You learned to look both ways. The world is a dangerous place and it is easy to get hurt. But you learned to manage to keep yourself safe.

At the same time, you continued to learn to manage your behavior. Hopefully, temper tantrums to get your way were no longer allowed. You had to negotiate with your parents and siblings for what you wanted. You learned how to be with your brothers and sisters, learned to play fair, to wait your turn, to say "sorry" when you had done wrong. You also learned to share. Most important, you had to learn how to calm yourself down when frustrated, learn to accept those limitations. Usually, you cried or even screamed in anger. Sometimes, you went back to a favorite blanket or a favorite toy. Sometimes, you still needed a parent to help you settle down after a frustration.

It is very helpful if parents have clear rules at home and you learn to accept them. Yet, some parents don't really have rules at home and the children battle it out; then they have a tough time learning what is acceptable or not. Other parents are too strict and their children are shy about getting involved with others. Abusive parents arouse fear and anger in their children. School, where the rules are clear and enforced, becomes difficult for children without clear rules at home, as they are unused to this new environment. Angry children are often bullies because they think it provides them safety. Fearful children are often their victims.

At school, children learn the very important rules of the classroom and the playground. You had to learn to get along with the other children. If you didn't, it really got in your way. You didn't make new friends. You were the trouble-maker in the classroom. Others tended to look down on you. You were the bully. Others feared and disliked you. Victims are often outcast. So, learning to get along was needed for a good experience in school. Unhappily, some children are not having a good experience in school and it takes them longer to learn to get it right. Still, they can get it right when they become aware of their mistakes, usually in the pre-teen years. You can learn to be a good friend and playmate, to be respected, even popular.

Most important, you started learning the more abstract rules needed to understand and manage in the world: arithmetic, reading, and writing. Even if you didn't realize it, those rules are the fundamental rules for playing in the world of adults. This was very important. It is challenging for most of us to learn the basic skills, but they are essential. In those late childhood years, your job was to get a solid grounding in those skills.

Ready for the Second Decade?

By ten years of age, you have learned the rules necessary to keep yourself safe and to prepare you for entering a world with all kinds of rules that allow people to live together in peace. You begin to enter the pre-teen years, preparing for the real work of the teen years: learning to become independent and responsible for yourself. It is important to take stock of where you are when you enter the second decade.

By ten years of age, you are expected to have basic skills in reading, writing and arithmetic. This is important. You can stop and evaluate where you were at the end of the first decade. You can also use the Identity Scale to measure yourself on the many qualities and social skills listed there; on the Behavior Scale, you can measure your behaviors that point to responsibility and autonomy. Together, they point to your confidence in yourself as you end the first decade and enter the pre-teen years.

Taking Stock

It is very important to be honest with yourself. You're in your private space. No one is judging you; don't judge yourself. This means you can look at the way you are without stating whether it is good or bad: it just is what it is. If you are aware that you are behind in reading or in math, it is most important to get the help you need to catch up as soon as possible. You already know that these are the skills that make you or break you – so get the help you need now! If you don't, life will become very hard and you will be tempted to give up, not have big dreams for yourself. But you can still catch up and breathe life into those dreams. I hope you will go for it!

 How to get help with basic skills in math and reading/comprehension. Most schools offer before-and-after school or lunchtime tutoring. There are also community programs that offer free help. Finally, there is the Web with programs such as Khan Academy that offer free help. There are many, many resources to help you at whatever level you are. Many school districts also have online lessons for all their classes, in order to help you stay on track. Everyone wants you to succeed – so get the help you need.

Managing Your Behavior

Just as important, is to understand where you are in your ability to manage your behavior. Are you able to accept rules and obey them to fit in the world? Are you able to manage frustration and other unpleasant emotions? Are you able to discipline yourself to attend to your work and your behavior?

Examples of Behavior Management

In the classroom: paying attention in class, asking questions, participating in class activities, completing your work, and avoiding disrupting classroom activities.

Outside the classroom: paying attention to time when going between classes. Making sure you have the right materials for class. Engaging with others during transitions and breaks in a friendly manner.

On the playground: participating in games, playing fair with others, obeying the school rules.

At home: do you start your homework without being made to by your parents? Do you get your homework done properly? Do you recognize when you need help and ask for it, either at home or at school? Do you make sure to have your needed supplies at home and that you take your work to school? Do you organize your bag and your papers? I see so many young people who have trouble with these skills. It is not unusual. You are not alone, but this is the time to get this worked out.

 How do you do this? Learn to chain events together, connect them to each other. What do you do when you get home? Do you put your school stuff in a corner? Are you hungry? Do you have a snack? Are you tired? Do you rest a bit? Are you restless? Do you go get some exercise? Do you want to contact friends? Call? Text? IM? So, you take a break.

Then, it's time to attend to homework. Do you get your stuff together? Did you bring home the books and assignments you needed? Do you need help? Do you know how to look it up? Do you get your work done? Is it done well enough?

How do you feel about it? Remember that this is not for your teachers or your parents, it is for you. This is for your life.

Do you organize your stuff to take it back to school? Get your bag ready for the next day? This is best done all in one stretch. Don't leave your stuff lying around to get messed up or lost. Don't leave the packing for the next morning. It is much easier to do it right away and be done with it. This way you won't forget it or misplace things.

This is how you chain things: do them in order, like the links of a chain. Snack/play first, then homework, then packing bag for next day. I often teach my clients to make a check-off list for managing their school work stuff. Do you need one? You could make one out of this exercise. Maybe add to it if you need. This would be good training toward being independent and disciplined (in charge) about taking care of yourself.

At home: do you attend to your chores without being constantly reminded? Do you keep your room clean and picked up?

 You can figure out your own list of chores and things you need to do at home. Then you can check them off as you get them done. That is often a good feeling. These are the skills that help people be successful (it is the little things that count): it helps you become independent, not picked on by others and reminded by your parents all the time.

Do you get along with your brothers and sisters most of the time? Do you respect them and your parents by not taking their stuff? Do you know how to accept discipline? Do you still throw temper tantrums if you don't get your way or did you learn to accept "NO" and manage your frustration by doing something pleasant for yourself? Doing something pleasant for yourself is very important. It helps you calm down, regain your balance, feel better. We call that "self-soothing."

 What things make you feel good? Some people go listen to music, while others just like to be by themselves. Still others chat with friends on their phone or computer. Some go outside and engage in some sport or go for a walk. It is important to have good self-soothing habits. Many people, even teens, like to eat when they're upset. This can become a problem very quickly. Others feel the need to drink or smoke weed. Or even do drugs. This is a much worse solution as it quickly creates very big problems.

So, behaviors that help you calm down and get back on track are very useful. Behaviors that calm you down but get you off track lead you away from your dreams and goals. This book will help you become aware of consequences and make the choices that you truly want.

You can attend to your responsibilities, which is also satisfying, though in a different way. When you get your work done, preferably well, you feel good about yourself. We call that responsibility.

These skills are so important that, if you are not there yet, it is very important to start catching up. You can often do it by yourself. Listen to that little voice inside you that knows whether you're doing the right thing or not. That voice may still be your parents' now but it will become yours as you grow up. You will be making these choices for yourself.

When I work with pre-teens, I often help them learn that these behaviors of self-care are now their responsibility and they take these on very quickly. Soon, they feel powerful and excited that they are becoming their own person, that they're in charge of themselves. Just like when they were babies, they have this great desire to keep growing. We all have that desire, even though it sometimes gets put aside for a while. This book will help you keep that desire squarely in front of you. You will seek to take care of yourself.

Chapter 3

New Skills Lead to:
Independence and Responsibility

Introduction

This chapter is the longest and probably the hardest; it is an overview of the rest of the book. That means that it will all be explained again in detail in the following chapters. In this chapter, you will be learning about the work of the second decade of your life (and even the beginning of the third). This is a very important time: it is where you are right now. Whether you are 13, 16, 19, or even 22, you are still in the period of adolescence. During this decade and some, you will be learning to become independent. That's a long time. There is no hurry. Life is lived one day at a time. Be patient with yourself but be also determined to keep growing. No one can avoid growing: it's an instinct, just as it was when we were growing in the first decade.

This is the decade where you grow beyond being a dependent child who looks up to parents, school, church, and community, to tell you the rules and take care of you. They taught and enforced the rules, rewarded you when you were following rules, and punished you when you didn't, so that you learned that those rules were essential to your success. You may not have liked the punishment, but it was essential. Parents had to take care of your need for successful behaviors and protect you from mistakes. Now it becomes your task to engage in successful behaviors and avoid mistakes.

Unfortunately, not all parents are able to teach and enforce rules, care for you, and protect you as you need. This is very unfortunate because it makes your life harder. But, now you can learn to help yourself! In this chapter and later chapters, you will read how you can learn to do that for yourself. That is because whether your parents were what you needed or not, it is every teen's job to learn to make their own decisions on how to live, to become their own person.

That means you will be learning to know and respect the rules, as they help you get what you want in life. You will learn to take care of your needs and protect yourself. This is what it means to become independent. By the end of the decade, as you do the work needed for your healthy growth, you will become independent, self-sufficient, and ready to go out into the world and succeed.

From Dependence to Independence: Pre-Teen Years

When I described the work of the first ten years, I showed you how it included learning to manage yourself in the world: learning the rules and, most important, learning to follow them even if it was hard. This included learning to manage your behavior even when you didn't like the rules. You learned to recognize your frustration and acknowledge it, but you taught yourself to go by the rules of society (we call that *discipline*). You learned that it feels much better to fit in than to feel like an outsider. The rules are there to make sure that we all fit in together, that we treat each other fairly and justly.

I know that some of you will think to yourselves that "there is nothing fair about the way the world treats me (or us)." You are right: racism and prejudice are most certainly not fair. Not fair at all! And they need to be changed. But the only way to change them is from the inside. To be on the inside to change them, you first need to go by the simple rules of fairness and honesty. It is the hard road, but the only road to your personal success and possibly making a difference for a lot of people.

Doctor Martin Luther King worked from the inside for many years, grounding himself securely, before he had the power and the following to be able to demonstrate and force changes on American institutions: look at the difference his work and his life made! President Obama has always worked on the inside and look at where he got! But here, too, these great leaders weren't alone and you are not alone. There are a lot of people helping to make change happen. Many people are ready to work with you, as well. It takes a long time. This can be frustrating, but an important part of these growing years is to learn that things take a long time; they take a lot of effort and they are done in little steps, every day.

Let's get back to your personal growth. Learning these basic skills is the most important. You may recognize that you're not so good at it.

Your emotions get in the way of your behavior. You feel frustrated, get mad, and want to give up on school and other work. It is most important to get that under control. "Yeah, how?" you may be asking yourself.

Read on. This book will help you choose between some good ways for you to change and some not so good ways. What makes them good or not so good? It is the way they impact your future. You have a future. If you want it to be the one you want, then you must take steps in that direction. Every day.

School work is frustrating. You may feel or know that you are behind. So, get help at school. There are tutorials before and after school. You will be surprised how much you can accomplish with a little help. There is also help online. Try it out. You are making steps toward your successful future.

Home life is frustrating. Start taking responsibility for your homework. It is not your parents' work. It is yours. It will go so much faster if you just get to it. Parents can help when it's difficult. If they are not able or available, for whatever reason, you can go on the Web. Sites like Khan Academy or K-12 will explain things carefully. Don't forget: every step you take can get you moving toward your goals and your freedom. When you start to get better grades on homework and tests, you will be surprised at how encouraged you will feel. You will see your efforts paying off. And they will keep paying off into your adult life. These are great skills for your future.

Another thing that now becomes entirely your responsibility is personal hygiene or care. Up to now, your parents may have reminded you to brush your teeth, shower, and shampoo, change clothes, etc. As of your tenth birthday, it is time to take that over. Like I mentioned in the previous chapter, if it's hard to remember, it is a good idea to make yourself a list to help you remember. You can then check things off as you do them. You'll soon know the routine by heart.

By the time you reach the teen years you need to be on top of this. Your friends and classmates are sure to notice everything and comment on it. Don't set yourself up for unpleasant experiences: take care to have enough time to groom and dress in the morning. Even if you are poor and have few clothes, they can be clean. You can learn to wash your clothes and even sew buttons, fix zippers, etc. These are good skills for the future.

From Dependence to Independence: Early Teen Years

The early teen years are from 13 to 15. You've already gained some independence and responsibility but, all of a sudden, you're asked to do a lot more. Your responsibilities at home are greater; your parents expect you to take on more chores. At school, you now have many teachers and you must move from class to class and manage to have the right stuff with you. That takes organization and planning. Your work at school is also much more challenging and catching up is becoming more difficult. All of this can feel challenging and frustrating and it is very important to learn to stay in control. That is the main work of the early teen years: learning to stay in control of yourself.

Remember that I wrote about self-soothing, taking care of yourself by doing something pleasant to help you recover from feeling frustrated, distressed or angry. When we learn this, we are unlikely to feel overwhelmed. We all have emotions. We all feel frustrated at times, or even much of the time. We learn to face and accept our emotions and then heal ourselves. Sometimes, just walking away from a troublesome situation works. Sometimes, we can't walk away. How do we manage frustration then? Can we just pull back in our minds? Just take a few deep breaths to help us regain our balance, our self-control? People used to say, "count to ten." That's the idea: put yourself on "hold" for a moment to decide how to manage the moment.

Maybe we can even wait till we have time to heal ourselves. We can listen to music, read, talk to a friend, go for a walk, get some exercise, play a game, watch a show, do things that help us feel better. This is a terrific way of taking care of ourselves. We get to feel in control of ourselves. Then, we can and must attend to what got us frustrated in the first place. All this was not an escape but a little rest and self-care so that we are not destructive in those situations or with ourselves.

Sometimes, young teens feel overwhelmed. That is when they may be at risk of being destructive, drinking or using drugs, running away physically or in their minds, fighting with others, or sometimes harming themselves. These things can soothe the pain for a bit, but then we must come back from a much more difficult place to take care of ourselves. You need to ask yourself this question: does this do something good for me or does it harm me? So, how do you figure that out?

Here it would be a good idea to use a decision tree (they are in the Appendix and online). Using a tree to look at your choices will right away help you feel more in control of your world. It will give you the foresight that you need and you'll be able to identify choices with good consequences that move you toward your goal of independence and responsibility, from those that do not.

 <u>Decision Tree example</u>: You are talking in class and the teacher singles you out by sending you to the principal's office. You feel it isn't fair because others were doing it too. You need to take a deep breath and decide what you are going to do.

<u>Decision tree time</u>. What do you do? Talk back to the teacher? If you do, it will only get worse. If you don't, you'll be afraid others will think you're a coward. What's more important? It is up to you. Do you want to look good to your classmates even if it gets you in more trouble with the school? Or do you want to get the least punishment you can? The first choice is for an instant goal; the second one is for a more long-term goal. It is up to you now that you've taken a moment to think it through.

Of course, you may not think it through as it is happening, but you can use this experience to plan for another time when you are tempted to act out in class, when you get caught acting out. You may also give some thought to where you stand with peers. What matters to you? Who is important to you?

This is also the time to learn to choose friends. Can you tell which friends are good friends and which are not? Do your friends take care of you in good ways? Do they respect you? Are they honest with you? Do they gossip behind your back? This is not an easy time and getting to know people is very important. It is most important to learn not to use people and not let them use you. A friend is not someone who befriends you in order to gain something, such as to get back at a former friend, use you to get into a group that's interesting, maybe make someone else jealous, or obtain favors or money from you.

This is, however, a time of trial and error. It is very difficult to know when you are being used and when you are being befriended in a genuine manner. Would you know if you do some of those things yourself? Respect is the most valuable thing that you can possess: that is, self-respect and respect of others. Sometimes, it is very hard to understand this.

If you have been respected in your home, you will know right away what feels right and what doesn't. If--and unfortunately this is quite common--you have not been respected in your home, it is much harder to tell between respect and the lack of it. Yet, you have that little voice inside you that I talked about before, which tells you when you are hurt by the way others treat you. You know when it is wrong for you. You deserve better and you need to insist on that. It may not be possible at home, but it is possible in the outside world.

This is an essential skill to learn to avoid being hurt, to avoid being used or misled by others and even by yourself when you do it to others. Of course, even if you are misled some of the time, you have the choice to learn from your experience and move forward. Now you know what to avoid. It is not easy, but it is what coping is all about. And you have learned to cope with difficult things before, like unfair treatment from sometimes difficult parents, perhaps.

But, remember, you are not doing this all by yourself. There are always adults to help, at home, at school, and in the community. In the following chapters, I will explain how you grow the skills that you need.

From Dependence to Independence: Middle Teen Years

The middle years are from 15 to 17. By now, you are more aware of yourself and of the things that you do. You're struggling with friendships and how to think of your future. Thinking about your future is most important. Believing that you have a future and that you can choose that future is most important. For some young teens, this comes easily. They have parents that have been talking to them about the future all along. These parents usually have a stable life and that future seems very possible to those teens even if they're not quite sure how to get there.

Most teens know that achieving in school is the key to a good future in this country. Most teens know that there is help if they have difficulties. They can ask parents, relatives, teachers, counselors at school, people at church, sometimes even neighbors and friends' parents.

But for some other teens, that future is very hard to see. These young people may feel hopeless about their future choices; they feel that they get no help or guidance from home. Sometimes, they feel they are so far behind in school that they will never catch up. These youths often decide to drop out when it gets too difficult. Or worse, they begin to take refuge in drugs so as not to face their fear and sadness about life.

But every single person has a future and can make that future better, whatever the circumstances. It is essential not to give up. "Where there's a will, there's a way" is the old saying. And it is true. Even if your home is very difficult and your parents are not helpful, there is help at school. Teachers are there, as well as counselors. And there is nothing they like more than lifting a young person out of despair or helplessness to a much better future. There is help in the community, at church, and from many volunteers. You only need to ask for it and you will get the help you need, even in the most difficult schools.

I know this because I have worked in poor, inner city schools. There were always people very devoted to helping kids succeed. They knew about school and community programs that could help. Yes, there is prejudice and racism but there are also people who are very fair and just. You can find them.

There are also psychologists in the schools: they are there just to help those having difficulties. Counselors and psychologists are there to help you find your path when you need it.

As you think of your future dreams, it is important to set goals for yourself. You know grades and school performance are the best ticket. A goal is to succeed in school to the best of your ability. This is a real challenge as there are many distractions and you have many other interests. So, how to keep it in balance? How to decide on priorities? What do you do first? How do you choose?

Here again, let's go to the decision trees and see how decisions, small and large, relate to your goals. You probably have more than one goal: maybe succeeding in school and going to the college of your choice is one. Another goal would be to be popular, to have a romantic attachment, to excel at a sport or two. Maybe excelling at a sport will get you into college with a scholarship. Maybe you also have responsibilities at home, like looking after younger brothers and sisters.

In the middle teen years, your life has become more complicated. You want to be more independent in making your choices, but you still need guidance as you're new at this. You need consistent rules at home and in the world of school and community. You basically know what is expected of you and now it is mostly up to you to decide how you choose to live your life. Which rules do you follow, which not? What are the consequences? What do they mean to you now and in the future? That future part is most important to think about.

The way to work toward goals is to think about the future as well as the present. As you grow up, you will learn that the future is often more important than the present. That is, we learn to put aside present choices for ones we will enjoy even more in the future. For example, going to a party tonight would be fun, but doing well on a test is going to be more rewarding in the long run. You probably know that the two options are not compatible, even if that thought is hard to face up to. If you go to the party, you will not be able to do some important studying and you'll be too tired and maybe hung over to study and do well on the test. If you skip the party, stay home and study till you're confident about the test; you will get a good grade and contribute to the grade average that will get you where you want to go.

Sha'anice's Story

Sha'anice knew there would be a big party on Saturday night at this popular girl's house. The girl's parents were going to be out of town and the party was a secret. Everybody was planning to go...But Sha'anice had a midterm exam in math on Monday morning. She was not doing too well in math, in fact, not well at all. She knew she'd have to work really hard over the weekend to do ok. What a dilemma. Sha'anice knew that school grades were very important for her mother who had great hopes for her future. Sha'anice's mom was a single parent who had never finished high school and she was determined that her daughter would have a better life.

This is a dilemma that teens encounter all the time. Sha'anice really wanted to go to the party. Her little voice said she really needed to get down to studying if she wanted to pass the math course. If she failed it, her mother would be really upset and disappointed. Sha'anice would probably have to go to summer school and this would be an expense her mother could ill afford.

Sha'anice really hated studying math. It was hard to understand. There was always so much homework. Yet, Sha'anice really wanted to go to college. She had a part-time job at McDonald's. It was so hot and tiring to work there. It was so boring even when friends came in. The thought of having to do that for the rest of her life if she didn't go to college just freaked her out.

Sometimes, she dreamed of getting married and becoming a stay-at-home mom but she knew that moms didn't get to stay at home anymore. They just worked even harder. So many moms weren't even married. Like her mother, they raised their kids on their own. Sha'anice's mom was a hairdresser pulling long hours, even on Saturdays. Her father had left the family years before. Sha'anice thought he worked as a mechanic at a gas station in another town. She remembered he had always been so tired and dirty with engine grease when he came home.

Sha'anice thought about the party. It would be so exciting. Everyone was going to be there. She could say that she had been there, too. Maybe there would be some weed. Everyone was going to be cool. Maybe, they could get into the liquor cabinet if the parents forgot to lock it. Or maybe someone would bring some from their home. How could she not go? She'd have to lie to her mother, tell her she was going to study with Beth at her house. If her mother knew anything about the party, she wouldn't let her go. She'd say: "no supervision, no party."

Sha'anice didn't have Decision Trees that would help her "look into the future." If she had worked it out, she could have made the choice that really fit her best. Instead, she argued with herself in her mind and did what we often do: give a big space for the easiest choice and a tiny space for the hard choice. Hard choices are just that: hard choices. It is much easier to think about something pleasant and exciting than something difficult and challenging.

Let's do a decision tree for Sha'anice. Please follow me (to the Appendix) and we'll lay it out. What it comes down to is this: What does Sha'anice want most for herself? Both choices seem to have good outcomes but one has the potential for a poor outcome and the other one doesn't. In other words, does she want to go enjoy the party, which actually might turn out badly if a neighbor calls the police, or might have poor consequences if Sha'anice drinks and is too tired or hung over to study, and so fails the test? That would make it even harder for Sha'anice to pass the course. Sha'anice might also make poor decisions about her personal safety and do things she might regret later. In any case her mother would be hurt and disappointed in Sha'anice's poor choice. Sha'anice, herself, might be sorry for her choice. What would the consequences be for Sha'anice? She might feel bad about lying to her mother and disappointing herself and her mother.

Avoiding the party in favor of studying would be somewhat painful for Sha'anice since she'd miss out on the fun. However, truly studying with a friend might be enjoyable and deepen the friendship. Those would be gains. She might improve her understanding of the material and gain in confidence to be able to succeed. She may well do OK on the test, therefore strengthening her position in the course. This would help her overall average and help toward going to college. Sha'anice would now feel good about herself. She could feel proud of her sense of responsibility for her own well-being. That little voice would give her all the confidence that she could succeed. She would also enjoy her mother being very proud of her.

Decision Trees help us be honest in our thinking about things. When we look carefully at the possible consequences of our choices, we learn to make decisions that fit us well. We feel stronger in our determination to take care of ourselves responsibly. Decision Trees can help us feel good about our life and confident in our ability to become the adults we want and hope to become.

Facing up to our inner thoughts, listening carefully to the little voice inside us that knows our true needs and our way, is crucial. Just like when we were driven to learn to walk, we are driven to take care of ourselves as best we can – this is what creates our happiness. We have all the answers we need within us. It is essential to listen to that voice: it is ours, it is us. I know that voice may often sound like your parents' as they are mostly doing their best to set you up on a good foundation for your life.

◆ ◆ ◆

At this age, you also have more responsibilities at home. Mostly, you may resent having to do chores, but these skills will help you when you are independent. In the future, when you'll live without your parents, it will be necessary for you to take care of all these tasks by yourself or with some others. It's good to learn that discipline, so that you know how to take care of yourself and your home.

But, in addition to doing chores, you probably have another, most important role at home: being with your brothers and sisters. How you manage your behavior with them is important. It is not unusual to have frequent conflicts with them. Do you demand fair treatment, respect, good boundaries, and do you provide the same for them? A good skill to learn is setting boundaries with siblings. This means that you stay on your side and request that they stay on their side. If you have separate rooms, it is easy: your room is your territory and theirs is theirs. If you share space, you can also insist on respect of your stuff and, in turn, you must also respect their stuff.

For some teens, this was achieved in earlier years, maybe during the pre-teen years. But for most, it is still a daily battle. It is a good opportunity to decide how you want to be treated and how you want to treat others. There are opportunities here for more than just battles and limit-setting. You can provide support and often valuable guidance to brothers and sisters. You can serve as a role model. If they are younger, you are their role model, whether you like it or not. They will likely pay close attention to what you do and follow it. So, it is a large responsibility to be in the position of setting an example. You could use it to encourage yourself to take very good care of yourself.

This will also affect how you engage in relationships outside of the home, at school and in the community. Will you expect respect and fair play? Will you offer the same to others? Many teenagers have trouble telling the difference between getting their way and treating others fairly and respectfully. They can be very charming and convincing. They pressure. Sometimes, they bully. They gossip, they even tell lies to manipulate people.

 Here is a situation you or your friends probably encounter all the time. Your friends want you to go to the mall with them. You know you have to get to your job on time because you've already been warned not to be late again. Your friends know that you can't go with them because you might lose your job if you're late again.

So, you tell them that you should go to your job. They make faces, looking like they are hurt and going to pout. You feel the pressure: you don't want to disappoint them and maybe get left out the next time. These are real concerns: you want to be popular. What to do? Is the voice saying that you will still get to work on time if you stay a while or is it saying that it will really squeeze you and you might be late again and make the boss angry with you? Most likely, you really would want to keep this job.

So, many times a teen is caught in exactly that type of scenario. Yes, your friends enjoy your company. But they will enjoy you just as much the next time. What if you go this time and then run late and get fired? Will you be upset? Maybe angry with yourself? Maybe angry with them for pressuring you? Will you blame them? It gets so complicated this way.

The best for you and them (in the long run) is to say with a smile "I'll go with you next time, but today I have to get to work." If they respect you, they will be just fine with this. Yet, they may tease you a little or pout, but that is ok.

In addition, you may not know it, but you will have set an example for them to put their own important stuff first. To be responsible. You will feel true to yourself and your needs. You will surely be rewarded with improving your standing at work if you arrive a bit early and impress your boss, taking you one step nearer to your goals.

If, instead of teasing you gently, they start putting on the pressure, maybe even threatening not to invite you the next time, then it makes the decision even harder. But only on the surface. You may feel frightened by their threats or you may get mad. In either case, this kind of threat means that they are not true friends: they don't have your best interest in mind. That's what a true friend is: one who cares about how well you are doing. True friends don't make threats if they don't get their way.

So, in this case, walking away as fast as you can is your best bet. It is hard and it may hurt, but these are not your friends. You may be disappointed and feel that you are alone. Maybe you can put those feelings aside for now and focus on your work.

At some point, you need to take some time to "lick your wounds," talk to a faithful friend or even a parent or a relative. You need to find something to bring you back to feeling OK. Sometimes music, sports, or some other activities help. Some teens use alcohol or drugs to feel better. This is very risky. It brings all kinds of dangers into your life. It will also largely keep you from attending to your goals for yourself, which, after all, is the reason you decided not to go hang out with those you had thought were your friends.

If you are paying attention to other people's negative behaviors, it can guide you to search for people who will treat you well. The way to tell the people that treat you well and respect who you are, is that "true" friends will not try to pressure you. Of course, they will want to get you to do things (everyone has needs and wants their way), but they won't insist if you don't want to. In addition, they'll still be your friends. That's the difference. They won't threaten to leave if you don't agree with them or go along. A good friend likes you "just the way you are", as the song goes. It may be cheesy but it's true!

Staying true to yourself is a very big challenge. It is one we all face, at any age, as there are always pressures to do things that may not be the best for ourselves. During the teenage years, it is especially hard, because teens want to be popular and included in things that they like. They like to be part of a clique so as to have a group around them. It is important to watch the clique carefully, as its members may put pressure on you to do things that you know are not a good fit for you. Remember: that little voice will tell you what fits and what doesn't. Clique members can put an enormous amount of pressure on members to conform. This is even truer of gangs where there is no room for disobedience. The rules are dictated.

Of course, it is better to avoid difficult groups altogether. Sometimes, you have already joined such a group. It is important to leave when it is not a good fit. Sometimes, it is very difficult and even dangerous to leave such a group. I cannot tell you here how to leave a gang. I don't know. It is often very dangerous. It is often extremely difficult to do it safely. I can only advise you to check very, very carefully, before you join a gang, because it is so dangerous.

Finally, as you learn to choose friends who are good for you, you also need to choose romantic partners who are good for you. This is very important to many adolescents. I promised you that I would not be lecturing on how far you should go in a romantic relationship. I will only urge you to apply the same rules to those partners as you would to friends. Make sure they are taking good care of you, not just of their own needs and wants. Avoid doing things under pressure or to be popular. Make sure you make decisions carefully and after using decision trees to examine your choices and their consequences. My advice: take care of yourself as well as you can and be responsible with those big decisions. It is often helpful to think about them and make those decisions carefully, ahead of time. Then you can take the time to explore how you feel about those choices, what you really want for yourself. The next time you are faced with that choice, you will have already decided what you will or will not do and it will be much easier to avoid getting caught up in the pressures of the moment, to stay true to yourself.

I have decided to talk here about gender identity and sexual orientation as this is very important to teens. Gender identity refers to whether you are comfortable in your gender, male or female. While most teens are comfortable with their gender, some are not. You may be confused, feeling more like a person of the other sex, at least some of the time. This confusion can be painful and difficult to deal with. No one wants to feel different from others, particularly during the teen years. Later, your gender identity or sexual orientation becomes much easier to accept and, hopefully, a source of pride in the person you are.

You all know the meaning of sexual orientation. While most teens are attracted to the opposite sex, some adolescents experience attraction to members of their own sex. If you have such an experience, you are aware of it, even if sometimes you try to avoid that awareness. It makes you different. Many teens can acknowledge that difference and face it. Many others wait till adulthood to acknowledge that part of their life.

Teens need to fit in and be part of everything around them; thus, differences of all kinds lead to insecurity. Teens are afraid to be made fun of or even shunned. Sometimes, teens are afraid of being attacked or treated aggressively by others for their differences. Homosexuality or gender confusion is very difficult for those who experience it. Most of these teens are having a very hard time with their private truth. In the past, it was almost always necessary to hide it in order to stay safe and accepted. It has become easier nowadays to acknowledge this struggle as being quite common. Yet, it is still difficult to face, to be true to one's reality, and to acknowledge it with parents and the community.

If you are bi-sexual, gay, transgender, or questioning, you no longer need to feel isolated. "Queer," "intersex," and "asexual" have also been added to the efforts to describe sexual identity. There is more and more support for you as a LGBTQIA teen or young adult, both in the community and online. There are also peers who share your challenges. In the community, there are counseling and support groups to help you address your personal concerns and deal with the practical realities of living in the wider community. Despite these improvements, one still has to be very cautious in many communities, as "different" teens may suffer from aggression from peers and from adults.

It is not always possible to come out to your parents, as much as you may want to. Many parents will be accepting and open about their acceptance. Many cannot and either may not want to know or will reject their teenage son or daughter. This is exceedingly painful. Teens usually sense whether their parents will be able to accept them or not. They need to prepare for the revelation or delay it. To prepare, they need to have support from friends, community, therapists, online support groups and contacts. If gay and transgender teens don't have enough support, they may despair in isolation and sometimes resort to harming themselves, or even committing suicide.

The responsibility we all have is to make room for everyone, whatever our differences may be. We have a responsibility to accept differences without rejecting or, worse -- hurting those of us who struggle with differences. Many states are struggling to pass non-discrimination acts to protect LGBTQIA citizens. I am sure that most of you are aware of this, since it is quite controversial in the world of adults.

As I encourage all teens to be true to themselves and to listen to that voice that guides them toward their future in the best way possible, I want to encourage teens struggling with being "different" to be true to themselves and face up to their difference. But I also want you to stay safe. You need to choose carefully those with whom you share your truth. I have already started explaining how to choose friends that are good "for the soul" and to avoid harmful people. This is to protect and preserve your true self. When you are faced with the difference of having a LGBTQ concern, it is most important to protect your true self.

You may choose when and with whom to share your truth so as to remain safe. There are many truths that you can't keep concealed and which, sadly, often lead to discrimination (such as physical characteristics, including race), but sexuality is fortunately something you can choose when and where to reveal, in order to take the best care possible of yourself.

From Dependence to Independence: Late Teen/Young Adult Years

As you enter the late teenage years, from 17 to 19, you're getting closer to becoming an adult. You're much nearer to independence, able to take on responsibility for yourself, managing decisions and their consequences so as to optimize (this means to make your life as good as possible) your life and meet your goals.

If you have done the work of the earlier years successfully, you feel more confident, knowing yourself. You're making concrete plans for your future. You may have decided to go to college and have a good idea of what you want to do "when you grow up." You may want to go to college to just keep on growing and learning, leaving it to later to decide on a career path. This is useful, too, as many teens don't know yet what they want to do.

Or it may be necessary for you to go to work right out of high school. Maybe you've already had jobs in the community and have begun to learn the rules of that world: how to work alongside others, how to manage orders, how to comply, how to be reliable so as to keep a job. You may have been forced to recognize and acknowledge your shortcomings and what you need to change to succeed in a job. You may even have started to learn what it takes to get ahead in your place of employment.

It's also possible to take college courses while working. Community colleges are good places to start taking college courses. They provide a lot of support and a chance to figure out what you want to do with a college education. They often offer courses to catch up on subjects where you need help, like math and writing. They also offer courses at convenient times for people who are working full-time outside of college.

In any case, this is the time when you need to feel more confident in yourself, and in your ability to succeed in the adult world. You've begun to learn to avoid pitfalls and temptations: how to choose between quick satisfaction or pleasure and long-term goals that allow you to succeed in the adult world, whether at work or college. You've come to realize that being respected and accepted for who you are is essential, that your positive decisions must be respected so that you can achieve a positive life.

You've learned to avoid peer pressure and choose friends that grant you respect and help you along your path, friends that you can help along theirs. There's a mutual appreciation and encouragement: you may have similar goals and want each other to succeed. These are the best friends: they help you keep your path in mind, help you feel proud and confident, help you feel that you're contributing positively to their lives, as well.

With this well-grounded self-confidence, you are becoming less easily influenced or distracted by temptations. You are more able to feel your center, your balance as you go through your day. You are making deliberate choices, weighing benefits and negative consequences of choices. You are feeling more independent and able to become an adult. What an incredible feeling of freedom you get when you are in harmony with your needs and your goals!

Now, you're also able to see things in a more detailed way: you can refine your choices. Here is an example:

Let's revisit Sha'anice's decision from earlier in this chapter. She is now 18 years old, a senior in High School. She has again a dilemma: an important exam to study for and an exciting party to go to. How to choose?

Sha'anice really has more than two choices. It is not just about whether to go to the party or study for an exam. As a young teen, she probably saw only two choices for herself. With more maturity, she would be able to see other options. For example, she could decide to go briefly at the beginning of the party and stay just an hour before getting to studying either by herself or with a friend. But Sha'anice knows herself well and she realizes that it will be very difficult for her to leave the fun. A better choice for her would be to study for a couple of hours first and then go to the party later, with no intention of studying any more that night. Sha'anice might also decide to avoid alcohol or pot so as to stay safe and be in good shape to resume studying the next day. This is a way for her to balance her needs. We all need to have time to relax and have fun even when we have lofty goals.

Balance is very, very important in life. We can and need to have time to relax and have fun even when we are devoted to our goals. I should say *particularly* when we are dedicated to our goals. We make decisions every day and we need to achieve this balance every day. No one works non-stop. We all need breaks. We need to reward ourselves for our effort and find time to take a break from effort to relax and rebuild our supply of effort-making energy.

It's not all or nothing: we don't have to choose only one or the other. But learning to make decisions to find the right balance for you is very important. This is a great skill to acquire for your life. It is part of developing the person you are becoming. Decision trees can help us see different options and their consequences. They allow us to have a look into the complex present and the future that awaits us. Everyday decisions engage us toward our future. Let's be wise in the way that we choose our path.

That positive feeling about yourself becomes your guiding light and helps you feel that you're living the good life: you're in sync with the world. Even adults often find it difficult to reach and maintain that feeling, but it is worth the effort. It is the feeling of happiness. It is the feeling of being true to your own self. It is the feeling that we all strive for and readily recognize when we have achieved it. It is a goal well worth striving for despite its difficulty.

As you strive during this period to become the person that you want to be as an adult, you need to activate and consolidate some constructive qualities that are essential to success. You are acquiring good skills for work or study as well as taking breaks. You have become aware of your strengths and, just as important, of the places where you need to make improvements to consolidate those strengths. You are aware of your preferences. This can be very challenging. Most people do struggle between easy choices and harder ones. We all do: that's what becoming an adult is about. It doesn't happen overnight. It still takes daily decisions.

Being able to consider choices and their consequences gives you great power. You use the Decision Trees and come up with clear options and are able to envision their consequences. This can enable you to make the best of what there is at each point. If you can do this, you are well ahead of many people who have difficulties with making positive or constructive decisions. There are temptations everywhere, but success depends on being able to manage the temptations as you keep your eyes on your goal. This is very straightforward, though it is also quite difficult for most people. But if you practice this crucial skill, you will find it much easier than it seems.

As a teen or young adult, you know how important your friends are. They are your whole world and they are the ones becoming adults at the same time as you. It is so important to be in the right situations, with the right people: that is the way to take care of yourself. Staying aware of what situations and friends work for you is one of the most important keys to success. Don't be easily swayed into behaviors that you wouldn't choose on your own if you were not being swayed. It is so important to avoid getting pulled into situations where it is particularly hard to stay on your path. But, remember it is always much easier to say no to a negative choice if you avoid being confronted with having to make the choice altogether. Look at what I mean with the example here.

An easy example: it is much easier to avoid eating ice cream if you don't go into an ice cream store or bring home a tub of ice cream. You can make life easier for yourself by avoiding the temptation altogether.

Here is a more challenging example. You need to prepare for work or for a test the following day and you know you need to go to bed at a reasonable time to perform well and stay out of trouble on your job or in your course. You're out to dinner with some friends and someone suggests going to their house to smoke marijuana. You have some choices to make now. Right now.

Do you go home after the restaurant? Do you go to the friend's house but tell yourself you won't smoke and you will leave early? How good are you with temptations? Do your friends put pressure on you to go along? Stay late? Get high? These are very common situations. They happen all the time. It takes some self-knowledge. What is easier for you? To leave after the restaurant? To go to the friend's and not smoke? To leave on time and get to bed so you can perform well tomorrow?

For most people, it's best to leave right after the restaurant. Don't forget that decisions are much harder when you're buzzed or stoned. For a very few, it is possible to have just one or two tokes and then go home. Most people who choose to go to the friend's house will not be able to stick to their wish to not smoke and leave early. Therefore, they will fail to keep their behavior in line with their goals. They will probably not do as well at work or on their school work the next day. They will probably feel bad about themselves. They will feel that they are too weak to really succeed. These are the self-disappointments that lead to lack of success and unhappiness.

Don't forget that you can find a good balance between having fun and being responsible to yourself. As a matter of fact, it is essential to make room for fun in order to take loving care of yourself. The fun just has to be measured and not be self-destructive.

As you near the end of your teenage years and enter young adulthood, you can be the person you want to be even when you are with others. You choose your friends carefully: they are the people who appreciate you for the way you are, who accept you for yourself, who do not pressure you into being any different, or doing their bidding. They are positive, just as you are and are intent on making good decisions for themselves (just as you are). They do not judge you or criticize you, though they may prompt you to stay on your path when you are having difficulties.

You have learned to avoid people who are unkind, jealous, envious, and maybe destructive. Unfortunately, others around you may be discouraged for whatever reason and engaging in destructive behaviors. This is sad for them, but the best you can do is to show them that one can be different. You can show them that one can take care of one's self and improve one's life chances.

Many times, teens that are kind and caring tend to get drawn into helping friends who are having a tough time and may even be acting in self-destructive ways. Trying to help them on your own is lovely and generous but it can also be very dangerous for you and for them. They often ask for your help and may want you to keep their problems a secret. This is wrong. The best way is to get an adult to help them. Later in this book, you'll be shown how to get needed help for yourself and for others who need it. Maybe this example will help you understand that teens and even young adults are too young to offer serious help. That is the job of the adults around you.

 Imagine you are on the shore and someone you know is in the water in difficulty. Maybe, they're even drowning. It's just awful. You want to jump in and help them. But before you do that, you need to estimate what you're getting into. Are you a strong enough swimmer? Are you strong enough to rescue them? Can you get help rather than do it alone? Will there be someone to help you if you get into trouble? Sometimes, it is

possible for you to help them on your own, but many times it might just be too dangerous for you both – leading to maybe two people drowning. Always remember that your first duty is to yourself. If you are drowning, you are of no use to anyone.

◆ ◆ ◆

In life, you must always take care of yourself first. This does sound "selfish," but if you don't, no one else will. When you were little, your parents took care of all your needs. Now, your job is to take care of your needs. For that to happen, you need to be aware of your needs and give yourself the right to meet them as well as you can. This is the rule for all of life. It is only when you take care of your needs -- and this can be quite challenging -- that you can be a positive person who can then help others.

If you've ever been in an airplane, you've heard the instructions: "if the oxygen masks come down, be sure to put yours on first, and then attend to others." When I first heard this, I thought this was so selfish and impossible: I would want to take care of my children first. But, no, if I pass out, I won't be of any use to anyone, not even them. So, it is essential to take care of myself first, to put the oxygen mask on myself first, so that I can help them.

So, as a mature teen or young adult, you see that it is essential to avoid those who get in your way. You avoid those who ask for too much from you or those who try to bully you into doing their will. You are in no rush to please others at your expense: this means you don't do things that you don't want to do. This can be about very small, daily things or about very big life decisions. You are in charge of your life. You are careful, taking care of yourself as well as possible, making thoughtful choices for your life.

You are very close to being independent and taking the best possible care of yourself. This may sound scary but it doesn't need to be. You know when others are treating you well. You even know when you are treating yourself well or not so well. That voice inside you is wholly yours now (not just your parents') and it guides you through your days. If you are lucky, you don't even hear it as separate anymore: it is a total part of you.

From Dependence to Independence:
Early Twenties/Young Adult Years

As we end the teen years and reach that magic age of 20, now comes the real test! Are we truly independent and able to assume responsibility for our decisions? Can we solve our problems alone or with help? Can we begin to think of taking care of others who will depend on us? Are we ready for committed relationships with romantic partners? In other words, are we ready for adulthood?

This guide book is geared primarily to those in the second decade of life, those who are beginning to learn the basic skills that propel us into independence, those who are preparing to answer those questions with "yes!" But, for many of us, the tasks of adolescence--learning to become self-sufficient, responsible, and independent—are still to be fully learned as we pass that magic number and enter our twenties. Many young people do not achieve true independence and autonomy until their early twenties or even later. For this reason, it has often been said that adolescence "carries" into the early twenties.

If you are a young adult as you read this book, you know that the skills to be mastered in this period are those you began learning earlier in your teen years. Now, your task is to mature these essential skills, and build self-confidence as you step into the world of adults. This work is of the utmost importance: there are now plenty of practical skills to be mastered as you enter adulthood. (I have listed several books in the Reading Recommendations to help you consider those skills).

For most young adults, this is an exciting time as they test their strengths in all the areas of their life and find ways to succeed. They forge their path to their goals, however challenging it is for them, building their skills and growing their autonomy; they gain self-confidence as they experience their own power and resilience in the face of obstacles.

Unfortunately, sometimes, young adults have been unable to build all the skills needed for their success during their earlier teen years, and are now experiencing difficulties as they enter their twenties. They have not been able to manage all the steps of adolescence, assuring their independence and autonomy. This can happen when there have been too many obstacles to their healthy growth and development.

Young adults may have difficulties hearing their own voice, identifying their path and goals, being assertive with others about their needs, choosing appropriate friends, gathering their courage (power) to thrive and succeed, and making positive decisions for their life. Instead of enjoying success, they are at risk of becoming depressed and losing hope in their ability to become their own persons.

If this is your situation, then, now more than ever, it is your responsibility to get the help you need to get your life on track and make it as good as possible. Help is always available. This is explained in detail in a later chapter. Never forget that everyone deserves a good life! You deserve a good life and you are the only person who can make it happen!

Chapter 4

Get to Know Yourself:
Find Your Strengths and Forge Ahead

So, we've now taken a good look at the first ten years and then a very close look at the work of the second ten years (and a bit beyond). You could be feeling that it looks a bit scary. There is so much to get done in that second decade, so much to learn. It does look like a lot, doesn't it? I guess it is hard to look at the whole ten years at once. But remember that 10 years is a very long time and we're all programmed to move forward and become adults. In some ways, we are even in a hurry. Many people want to try out adult things very early on. They want to try sex, tobacco, drugs and alcohol, maybe even running off and making it on their own. But, my best advice is not to hurry, to just take your time, to get there in the best way possible.

If you're a young adult as you're reading this, then you might be thinking that all this is doable but if you are a younger teen reading this, it might well feel like way too much. You can't even imagine learning all those things and becoming an adult. That is perfectly normal. It is still far away. In these next chapters, we're going to look at how to do all that work of growing up, one step at a time.

First, it's important to figure out where you are now. How old are you? How do you describe your personality on the Identity Scale? How do you rate your behaviors on the Behavior Scale? How do you feel about them? Where are you seeing your strengths: those parts that you enjoy most? Where are you lagging behind where you want to be: those parts that you'd like to improve? It is most important to enjoy those aspects of your life that are going well. You can be pleased with yourself. Those are assets. They are valuable. They give you strength.

It's also important to understand *why* you are doing so well in those areas. How did you build those skills? Maybe they came naturally and you never thought about them. But look more closely. Let's say you are good at sports. If you're good, it is likely that you put in a lot of hours practicing. You probably didn't mind because you enjoyed it, but that was a lot of time anyway. You wanted to be good at what you were learning. You wanted your skills to be good. If you were weak in one area, you worked at it until you got it. Good for you!

Well, that's what it takes to have good skills at anything. No one is born with those skills. They must be acquired. Our strength grows when we build good skills for our life. So, look at those areas where you'd like to improve. How do you get better, nearer to your goal for yourself? Start small and practice, practice, practice. If you have a challenge, then you need to look at it closely. If you can't do something, then get help from family, from a coach, from school, from your church or community, or on the Web. Stick with it. You will begin to improve and see that you can do it. It will feel good. It might even become one of your strengths. It doesn't necessarily take genius to do something, but you do need to stick with it until you get it. Just like the infant trying to walk. There is no baby who decides it's too hard and just doesn't ever learn how to walk. (Even babies with severe handicaps do their best to learn to walk or at least move around). You may laugh at this as an example, but what we are talking about here is really no different. Skills allow you to walk through the world.

I hope that you use the Identity and the Behavior Scales here to take a close look at where you are and what is important to you. That awareness is the key: you are building your identity, the person you want to be and the person that you want to present to the world. That first part is about knowing yourself and, most important, accepting who you are. You may want to improve on some things, but first you need to understand where you are and accept that, without judging yourself. You are you. You know where you are now and you know where you would like to be as you mature into adulthood.

This knowledge is going to be your guide. This is what allows you to set your goals. This is what you keep in mind as you work your way toward your goals of accomplishing your dreams. This is the base. You may be thinking that you don't have any dreams. But everyone has dreams. Your dreams are there and you need to be aware of them to make them happen. Maybe, you have forgotten about them because of other difficulties. In this case, it is even more important to remind yourself of your dreams and to establish goals.

Maybe you are afraid your goals are not realistic: they are "just" dreams. Some people believe that growing up means giving up on their dreams and being "realistic." Nothing could be further from the truth. Giving up on dreams leads to feeling defeated, to feeling like a failure. No one deserves that. This is when you certainly need to get back to your dreams. It is likely to be a big (maybe a very big) struggle to make them happen but trying is much better for you than giving up. Life is not about giving up. So, I hope that even if you are discouraged from realizing your dreams now, you will reconsider and give yourself the chance that you deserve.

You may feel that there is just so much work to do just to start making a dream happen. Maybe you are very far behind in school skills. You will be surprised how fast you can catch up when you set your mind to it. It starts small, but then you discover that there are already so many things that you have learned, that you can do. It gets bigger fast. You learn how to help yourself, how to get help from others, how to keep moving forward. There are so many stories of people who have braved many obstacles to succeed. Everyone can join that group of people who struggle to get ahead. You have no idea how far you could go. It might take time. Sometimes, it even takes more than one generation, but you can make it happen.

Think of people who have had a very hard time of things and yet made a great life for themselves. Actor and Comedian, Jim Carrey was homeless as a teen, but look at where he is today! One of our Founding Fathers, Benjamin Franklin dropped out of school at age ten, but went on to forge his own path to incredible success, not only as an inventor, but as a politician! Oprah Winfrey was horribly abused as a kid and became a teenage mother; yet, she has carved for herself an impressive piece of the pie! Abraham Lincoln grew up in poverty and lost his mother when he was a child; yet, he forged a very significant path for himself. Where would this country be without him? Jay Z couldn't get a record deal but, like so many artists, he kept going and created a new path for music. Charlize Theron's mother killed her father in front of her when she was fifteen. Despite this devastating trauma, she forged on to create a fine career for herself. Maya Angelou was severely abused as a child and had a very difficult early life; yet, she went on to become an important voice in America. She was a poet and Civil Rights Activist and was awarded the Presidential Medal of Freedom by President Obama in 2011!

 Remember the story of First Lady Michelle Obama. Her father took care of the family and instilled in his daughter a great deal of ambition. He had started the family's dream and he understood that Michelle might be the one to really move the family's dream forward. Many immigrants, too, are focused on preparing the next generation for advancement.

My own family was like that. My parents brought us to the United States and they both worked very hard so that my sister and I could go to college. We didn't go to an expensive college. In those days, City College of NY was free if you had the grades to get in. What better way to encourage young people to work hard? My parents worked hard so that we could go to college full-time and prepare for our careers. We held only small jobs on the side to pay for books and lunch money.

This is how families pull themselves out of poverty. You prepare the path for your children and teach them to want something better. Hopefully, your parents have been doing that for you. If not, you can do it for yourself and for the next generation.

As you work toward the future, having the strength to look at the places where you need improvement, maybe a lot of improvement, takes a lot of courage. Courage: A most important quality –doing something even when it is scary or it seems very difficult. (On the Identity Scale, there is "Courageous/Discouraged").

I hope you can find your courage or grow it, if needed, because it is the key to your success. People who win do so because they are able to overcome obstacles, often very big obstacles. But remember that it is not done all at once. We take on just a little at a time, a very little bit at a time. The saying "A journey of a thousand miles starts with one step" means that you only need to take one step at a time. You have a lot of time and each little step is not that scary. You already know how to overcome obstacles: you keep at it till you get it, doing the things you are afraid of one step at a time.

So, let's look at the areas that are important to young people. Probably the most important is to feel that you are doing well in the social realm. You want to find friends that you like and that treat you well.

You want to be a good friend as well. You may need to learn how to be treated with respect and how to treat others fairly and with respect, so that you feel good about yourself; you want to find equally good people to build friendships with. In a later chapter, I will help you learn how to do just that.

You likely want to have power in your community. That means that you want to be respected and maybe you want to be a leader as well. You don't want to be bullied or left out of social activities. It is so important to you to find your role, that you put a lot of your energy toward that goal. This is true particularly if you are a young teen and are trying to figure out the person (your identity) you want to be in front of others. This consumes many young teens and it is, indeed, very important to figure out your status in the community. It is also possible to make very costly mistakes such as joining gangs or engaging in very dangerous activities to prove yourself. I will write about that in more detail in a later chapter.

It's important to realize that you pick and choose your role every day. You can change it over time as you grow up. For example, if you were the class clown in elementary or middle school, you don't have to keep it up in high school. You are free to change to an image that suits you better now. As a matter of fact, we all change over time and it is not so good to stay stuck in something that was good earlier but may not be so useful or desirable now. If you go to your Identity and Behavior Scales, you can see that you change over time and that you can choose the direction for that change. You have preferences and ideals: I encourage you to look at them closely and keep them in mind as you grow through this period and the rest of your life.

Another area of challenge is school learning. This is a very important one, though like most teens, you may have a tough time figuring out why this is so important. Even if you are planning to go to college and know that good grades are needed, it is hard to understand why it matters that much. Yet, it does matter very much.

Grades measure what you know: adults need to know a lot of things to be successful. Everything is about learning to do things, from fixing a car to programming a computer, to teaching others, or being a doctor who takes care of people's health. So, if you are finding yourself behind or just in difficulty with the current school work, it is most important to figure out ways to catch up. There are many ways open to you, but it is entirely up to you to seek them out and take advantage of them. The longer you wait, the harder it becomes. Some people fear that it then becomes too late…but it is never too late to help yourself. You can always pick up from where you are now to make your life better.

Even if you have no plans to go to college or even finish high school, you need to realize that the more you know about life and the world, the more money you can make in jobs and the easier your life can be. If you can be a person who is going to learn what is needed to get ahead, then you will be getting ahead and making yourself a better life. Also, you know that it is never too late: even if you leave school without graduating, you can finish the work later; you can even go to college on a scholarship. There are ways to get ahead for people who take the time to find out how. It is always there: it is just up to you to decide and to find out what you want for yourself.

Yes, it does tend to become harder if you don't follow the easier path (of going on to college right away) but for many people that path is not available to them when they are in high school, due to their circumstances. Many times, there are things already in their way. But think of the people I mentioned before who had so much in their way when they were young and yet forged a different and successful path.

This is a very important life lesson. It is always up to you what you do to help yourself get a good share of things. No one else can do it for you. Yes, it is true that some kids have it easier because their families can offer a lot of help, but everyone can have access to community and school resources. That too will be further explained in a later chapter.

A really important area of challenge is how you feel about yourself. How do you see yourself when you use the Identity Scale? The Behavior Scale? What changes would you like to see happen? That means what changes would you like to work toward? Because, remember that no one can do it for you. Are you satisfied with the way you look? With the way you act around others? Are you OK with your behavior at school or in the community? Are you OK within yourself about your behavior? Do you feel good about the way you are in the world? This is what this book is about: how to take care of yourself and be the person you want to be, now and in the future.

Finally, one of the biggest challenges is at home. Why is that? Home has the people who know you best. Probably, you used to be comfortable with them. They understood your needs. However, now you just can't stand your parents' demands and they sure don't seem to understand your priorities. This is pretty much normal, unfortunately. You surely wish they did understand. Maybe, you often wish they would just leave you alone and let you lead your life.

The Importance of Separation

The work of your teen years is to separate from your parents so that you learn to lead your own life independently by the end of adolescence, by the time you are an adult. This is really very difficult. That's why you have so much time to get it done. Think: you learned to walk in just a few weeks. You learned to talk in a few months. You learned basic reading and writing in a couple of years. But you have at least ten years to learn to become an adult. More time means much more to do and much more difficulty.

Don't forget that just like when you were a toddler, you are now very eager to become an adult even if it is really scary to think about. Just like a toddler, you have a natural drive to do that growing into adulthood. Yes, there is much friction at home as you learn to move ahead, but you do it anyway. That friction is normal. Your parents are having a hard time learning to let go and giving you the *right* amount of freedom and responsibility, and you are struggling to free yourself of their influence and their domination. I said the right amount of freedom and responsibility because it is your parents' job to make sure that you don't have too much freedom or responsibility for yourself and lose your way. Unfortunately, sometimes parents give too much freedom and then it is very hard for the teens to find the right paths. They risk getting lost and encountering a lot of difficulties.

Most parents are hard at work gauging just how much freedom you can handle. They need to keep the rules firmly in place so that you can feel safe. Even if you are disobeying the rules at times, it is necessary for you to know that they are there, that there are consequences to disobeying the rules. This is to prepare you for the adult world. There are many rules in the adult world and the consequences for disobeying are sometimes quite harsh. A lesson you would do well to learn when you are still at home: your parents are trying to protect you from the rigors (or consequences) of the adult world.

Most parents are very diligent, which means very much on top of things: watching out for your safety, for your having just the freedom you can handle. But, sometimes parents don't know how to do this for you or they are just too busy to attend to this part of your growing up. If parents are just not there to limit your freedom, you may be in danger of losing your way. When parents are not there enough, it is your job to take over and limit your own freedom so as not to lose your way.

You may think this is impossible but it's not. As you learn to listen to that voice inside you, the voice that is your true guide, you will have a good idea of what will work for you and what won't. If you're honest with yourself when you use the Decision Trees, you can make very good choices. Then, you can limit your own freedom to what you know you can handle. Sometimes, the voice is loud and you have no trouble following it. Sometimes, it is quiet or just confused, and you tend to experiment to find out what works for you and what doesn't. This is the harder path but it is still a good one as you benefit from what you learn about yourself.

<u>Here is an example of parents setting clear boundaries</u>. Parents need to have clear rules for their children. Those rules need to be appropriate for the children's ages and abilities and they need to be enforced consistently. Rules are only useful if they are enforced and the teens can count on consequences when they violate the rules. A good example is having a clear curfew for teenagers. It should be a reasonable time, usually decided by the parent. Parents should resist pressure to go beyond the time that is reasonable for them and their teens. The curfew time is known to both the parents and their teens. The consequences for violations are also clear to both the parents and their teens and are always enforced if there are violations.

In my home, teens were not allowed out on school nights, which included Sunday evening. On weekend nights, they would be picked up by 10 pm. Sleepovers were often arranged when they were too young to drive; however, sleepovers' bedtime was still 10 pm. After 16, the curfew was set at 11 pm; I set the house alarm at that time and went to bed. They could not sneak in without waking me up. They could arrange for sleepovers ahead of time.

After 16, the local police curfew was 11 pm and my children were instructed that if they broke the law and were caught, they would spend the night in Juvenile Detention. I would not come during the night to bring them home.

This worked well. There were no violations that I know of (this is important: I didn't have to know everything, only the major difficulties). The police never called. My children did have a good social life, stayed with friends if they wanted to party. We had many parties at my home with sleepovers. I think it worked out OK.

On the other hand, not all parents can provide such supervision with consistent rules, particularly if they are frequently absent from the home due to work or other reasons. This one is more complicated because there are many reasons that parents may be absent and not helpful to their teenage children. Some are just too busy and don't have time or energy to attend to this most important task. This is very sad for the teen. If this is your life, I am sure that you feel their absence very sorely; you may even be angry with those who are not there for you when you need them. The truth is that even very busy parents can be there if they know how to. It doesn't take much time to set rules for children and to make sure they understand their purpose and observe them.

The problem is that often those parents who are not so good at parenting didn't get the discipline (that means the rules and boundaries) from their own parents, because their parents didn't know how to do it either. Just like parents who don't know how to read or write well feel that they can't help their children (this is not true – fully illiterate parents can encourage their children to get the skills they didn't get), many parents feel helpless to teach discipline and obedience to their children because they never leaned it themselves. Sometimes, they go overboard and are super strict, but too often they just give up and figure that their children will find their own way. Sometimes, parents expect the schools to take care of this part of raising their children. This makes it very hard for the school and for the youths and they often go on struggling with these challenges past their teen years.

So, what happens when children and teens are not taught discipline at home? Often these children have great difficulty managing themselves. They can become angry and act out, bully others, get in trouble at school or with the law; sometimes, they even head for drugs, gangs (which have very strict rules), and some criminal activities. If they are really out of control, they often get into jail, where they finally have the rules and limits that they need to know how to behave. Many people keep returning to jail because they don't know how to manage in the free world; they feel safer in jail.

Other teens become depressed and have a tough time making their way forward. They might get into drugs or alcohol to soothe their anxiety and depression. Sometimes, they are lucky and can figure out for themselves a path such as doing well in school because school feels safe and the rules are clear and useful. Sometimes, they do it with help from teachers and counselors.

But remember that everyone can succeed. Here are two examples of women who grew up being terribly neglected by their parents. Yet both managed to make better lives for themselves.

 One woman was abandoned from very early on. Her mother left the family and her father kept the children at home but he was hardly ever there. He did provide food most of the time. This woman, at the age of 5, took care of her brothers and made sure everyone went to school. She took on this responsibility all by herself. Of course, she didn't have much of a childhood but she did manage to take care of herself, succeed in school, put herself through college, and later have a career.

The other woman's parents separated when she was little and then kept taking the children from each other and then leaving them with their own parents, the children's various grandparents, where they were poorly supervised and frequently abused. This woman attended ten different schools but she stuck it out. She graduated from high school, went to college and went on to have a career!

Both these women come to me for help because it has been very hard for them without the guidance of parents and they are never quite sure of themselves -- every decision and every step is a challenge. Yet, they are both upstanding people who are fair and just with others, good citizens who have made a life for themselves despite their problems.

When I worked with children inside and outside of the schools, there were many who were struggling with homes that were disorganized and even chaotic. I think some of you may be struggling with challenges like that now and this may sound very familiar.

But whether you can get the help you need at home or not, the important piece is that you can become aware of what you need as you enter the teen years, and much earlier for some. You can learn to build those skills for yourself. You know the rules at school and in the community. You are learning the way to do things. This book is to help you learn to make decisions for yourself. All teens must learn this as they grow up since they have to learn to replace their parents, whether their parents have been very present and helpful or not. There is help for this everywhere: at school, in the community, and in religious institutions. Guidance for this learning is offered everywhere.

So, as you learn to look at your needs and you decide how you want to start helping yourself, using the two scales and the decision trees might be useful in helping you move forward in areas where you may be feeling behind or stuck. I think that they could help you put your ideas down on paper and see what your options are. Remember that you start with very small steps. Use the blank decision tree and see if you can identify the steps, at least a couple of them. You manage one thing at a time. Remember, it is important to take your time to succeed -- a little bit at a time.

Let's take a small example: say you're afraid of speaking up in class. A lot of teens feel afraid that others will think they're dumb. But smart people ask questions, a lot of questions: they want to learn. They feel entitled to explanations: that's what they're in school for. If you ask questions, you are showing others that they're owed that education.

You can use a decision tree to help you decide on what behaviors you could choose. One is you can do nothing or you can try something. Do you have choices open to you? Yes, you do! You can start with deciding that today you will say one thing in one class. See how it feels. Most likely, it will be ok. You will feel proud that you did it. At least a little proud. Then tomorrow, you can move up to two times a day. Or, maybe, you can go ask the teacher a question after class. You can even go to the tutorial session before or after school where you could ask more questions and get more answers that will give you confidence. Before you know it, you will have gotten over your shyness and ask questions or give answers whenever you feel like it. Done! In addition, you will feel much more comfortable with the subject matter. Success! You will realize that you are much more powerful than you thought you were. Your life is now going in the direction you want and you can go back to the Identity and Behavior Scales and see where you might place yourself now. Maybe you put Speaking in Class, or Asking Questions When Needed, as behaviors that are important to you. These scales are there to be mirrors for you, to help you look at your needs.

A more challenging example: you might be shy in social encounters. That's more complicated, but here, too, you can take little steps. Here, you must first identify your fears. What are you afraid of? What has happened in the past to make you afraid? This is important. Think about a negative incident. What happened? Some people are afraid to be laughed at, mocked, or teased. Some are afraid of being rejected or even bullied. So, they feel they never know what to say. Others fear that they are boring or silly.

How about caring less if any of these happen? Sounds weird? Well, yes. But when something negative happens, it can teach you something about yourself that is very valuable. While it is painful to be thinking that you said something dumb, you might also think about what you wish you had said to prepare for next time. Next time, give yourself a tiny moment to think about what you really want to say. Give yourself permission to say it. This is quite a bit like speaking up more in class. It just takes practice.

Here you can use a Decision Tree to look at what has already happened. It is often a good idea to use Decision Trees to see what happened in the past, where we made choices that brought on difficult consequences. This might be difficult but being honest with ourselves as we look at our choices can be very useful in deciding what choices to make in the future.

You can go over what you said and what happened. Could you have said something different? How do you think that would have worked? Usually, your voice will tell you what you wanted to have said or done. Sometimes, the doing is walking away when you are not treated well or with respect. That is an answer too, a very loud one. Sometimes, you will need help with facing someone who is particularly difficult. Maybe there is someone who can help you work it out: a parent, older sibling, teacher, school counselor, or even a therapist. There are also books that will help you come across as you want.

The Power of Anger

Maybe you are angry, angry about a lot of things. Angry about the way things are at home, angry with the schools, angry with the community. It is normal to be angry when your feelings are hurt, when you feel left out, neglected. People can be angry because they are poor, because they feel that they are discriminated against as a people. This is often a very righteous anger. You are right to be angry. What is most important is how you are going to use that anger. Anger gives a lot of energy. It can be very useful.

I am writing this at a time when there are a lot of riots in American cities where African-American people feel that they are being victimized. They are, of course, totally right in protesting unfair treatment in their community but riots rarely promote lasting changes. Hopefully, people will also feel more motivated by their anger to accomplish more lasting changes. The way to do that is to succeed and make changes from the inside. Of course, President Obama is the perfect example. But you don't have to be President of the United States to make changes to the world. Everyone can make changes.

How will you use your anger? Hopefully, you will want to make a better life for yourself. This means using that energy. But be careful here: there are many choices. You can use it to be vengeful and destructive, but we both know that will get you in an awful place where your future will have little chance of being what you want. Or you can be angry at what you consider your fate and become hopeless and self-destructive, doing drugs and alcohol. That also takes you down a very sad and difficult path.

I hope that you don't see these choices as being the only ones open to you. You have many others. You are entitled to a piece of the pie. Go and get it. Work your way to the table. You can get the skills you need even if you are behind in some areas. Or even behind in all areas. Remember, even if you have dropped out of school or are about to do that, you can always go on and get back on track. Just don't give up!

Just this morning, I was reading that the brain will do what you ask it to. You're in charge. If you desire to understand math, get better at reading, or pitch a baseball, or whatever, your brain will head that way. If you want to give up and remain angry and hopeless, then your brain will take you in that direction. This was very exciting reading for me: it explains why, once you make a small effort and move forward, you gather speed quite quickly. It is that first step that is the most difficult. The decision is up to you.

Here the decision trees again help you to examine your choices. They help you give yourself a chance even if you are feeling discouraged. Go for it. Decide to do something, see where it gets you. Then do another small thing, see where that leads you. Before you know it, you are closer to your dream: it feels more real. Will you allow yourself to gain speed, to make things unfold in the direction you truly want? I hope that you will regain hope and find your direction if you are a person who fears that the pie is not for you.

Example: Jason, a teen in the shelter

Many years ago, I volunteered to work with teens in a shelter. Most of these young people were angry and some were even quite depressed. One boy was very angry because his girlfriend was in the hospital and he couldn't get information about her health. He had called twice and been told he couldn't talk to her. He had slammed the phone down in anger.

I sat with him and listened to his frustration and fear that she wasn't doing well. He clearly loved his girlfriend deeply. When he had calmed down, I asked what went wrong on the phone. He had demanded to talk to her and slammed the phone down when told that he couldn't talk to her. He was then invited to review what his choices were. Like using a decision tree. You can continue with something that doesn't work or you can explore what might work. What if he sounded calm and polite, in control of himself? Could he get to talk to her? He agreed that it was worth a try. He agreed to rehearse with me. He would place the call, introduce himself calmly, and request patiently and politely to talk to his friend, stating her full name in a "mature" fashion.

Guess what? He did as he had practiced and got her on the phone after waiting a few minutes! First time around! Could he have done it on his own? Maybe not. But this is what this book teaches you to do. As you work on your choices and your self-presentation, you can get the results that you want.

Finally, how useful was his anger? It gave him the courage to sit with me, a total stranger, to vent and go over the problem. It gave him the courage to examine his behavior. Then, it gave him perseverance to look for a solution to his problem, keeping his eye on the goal. It also gave him the drive to keep trying till he succeeded. All in all, it gave him the energy to struggle for what he really wanted.

Here, I want to point out that emotions are and can be very useful. They tell you how you feel about what's happening to you or around you. You need to know how you feel. So, you learn to recognize your emotions and put them into words for yourself. Then you can decide how to use these emotions to make your life better. You have a choice: you can respond positively and move forward or negatively and slow yourself down. (I will talk about this in much more detail in the next chapter). That means you can believe in your own goodness, like Jason in the example above, or you can despair, not believe in your power, like he felt before we had talked. It was all in how he saw himself.

So, it is all in how we see ourselves. We are all good and we can all find our own resources: they are there, deep down. We just need to look carefully, particularly when we don't believe in our own goodness. But it is there: keep looking until you find it. Everyone deserves a good life; you can decide to make a good life for yourself even if you are unhappy and angry most of the time. Just like that boy, you'll be amazed at the change once you feel liberated from this fear that there is something wrong with you, that you don't deserve better.

My wish for you is that you look carefully and find your strength, your goodness, and move forward to make yourself the best life you can. You deserve it. Everyone deserves it. That is how we make the world a better place. That's what it takes: one person at a time, each day, striving to make their life good and happy.

Chapter 5

Learn to Live with Your Emotions: Manage Your Behavior

In this chapter, I will be writing about how to live with your emotions and manage your behavior. I gave a hint of that in the last chapter. You may be angry, but you also have the freedom to decide what you will do with that anger. You have choices. For you to have those choices, you must first become aware of your emotions and name them! Then, there has to be a little "space" between emotion and action. We call that awareness; it gives you choices. If we are not aware of our emotions, then we cannot choose our behavior. When we only react to situations, when our buttons are pushed, we do not have control. That is very much to our disadvantage. It feels as if others can control us.

We need to be aware of what we are feeling. We feel an emotion first. We feel it physically. We blush. We shake. We feel our heart beat faster. We feel hot. We clench our fists. All those are sensations related to our feelings. They can be overwhelming if we don't make the effort to name them. To name them, we need to become aware of them.

When you were a child, you experienced your feelings. It was often your parents who labeled them for you. They asked "why are you upset? Angry? What happened?" They helped you make sense out of what you were feeling. As you grew up, you became able to name your emotions for yourself, to understand what you were going through. You could tell others just how you felt.

Your parents may also have helped you separate your emotions from your behavior. "I know you're angry with your brother, but you may not hurt him." They told you that you had a choice on how to manage your behavior. There were expectations that you could manage your behavior. In school, it was most important to choose your actions so that you could avoid unpleasant consequences. Teachers went out of their way to teach fair play, apologizing properly, making amends. They encouraged you to manage your behavior and take responsibility for it.

As you enter the teen years, it is good to have the basics of this self-management under control. However, it is likely to be still very hard for you to acknowledge your emotions and keep your behavior under check. People are always telling you to "control your emotions." That is actually inaccurate (wrong). We don't control emotions. It is important to know that emotions are natural and generally correct. They tell us how we feel about what is happening to us. We are happy when treated well, sad or angry when treated poorly, and afraid or angry when threatened. We know whether what we are getting is fair or unfair treatment. Our little voice is always telling us.

The important piece is for us to recognize and accept our emotions. We need to trust in them. Being aware of our emotions, of how we feel about things and people at any moment, is very important. Our emotions are our antennas to sense the world around us. However, many teens don't recognize their own feelings, their emotions and, therefore, cannot choose their behavior at the time; only afterwards, do they realize "Yeah, I got angry and struck out." **Once we reach adulthood, the ability to be aware of our emotions and choose our behaviors becomes essential to being in command of ourselves and successful in life.**

Acting and Reacting

Many teens do not realize that they have a choice. Learning about adulthood is learning that we have a choice about how we act. I say act because many people, young and old, only react to events. This is a very difficult concept that I am going to explain here: many people allow others to "push their buttons" and they often react with fear or anger and strike back, almost like a reflex. This kind of impulsive reaction is normal for young children. They do not realize that they have a choice in how to respond.

Take note here: we all want power. Those people who are in charge of themselves, who choose their behavior and don't just react rashly, without thinking, they are the winners. They are the ones who are in control of themselves and the world.

We can learn to choose our answers and our responses to events carefully. Sometimes, we even plan a script when we anticipate a difficult encounter. There is nothing wrong with being well-prepared, like Jason (in the last chapter), the second time around.

I want to share a funny example from a movie. Of course, it's not very realistic but it does make the point. This nine-year old boy stuttered and, of course, was picked on and bullied. He did put up a good fight against four boys but ended up losing, of course. He was very upset and angry. He didn't want to tell his mother what happened, but his sister did!

The next day, an old family friend told him of a trick to scare the boys and his sister helped him carry it out. On the way to school, she went to the boys that were waiting for her brother and warned them that he goes mad when he gets angry. Of course, they just laughed. But he put something in his mouth that foamed and ran up to them, acting crazy and drooling like a rabid dog. They got scared and ran off! They, of course, left him alone from that day forward.

The lesson is this: at first the boy just reacted to the bullying by fighting even though he knew he couldn't win. He walked away with a black-eye, feeling frustrated and angry. After admitting to the defeat, getting help, and making time to plan what to do to win, he was more successful.

I must point out that the boy's trick was harmless. I am not suggesting any kind of violence toward others.

The difficult piece for all of us is what to do with our emotions. How do we respond to our feelings? Do we react immediately or do we wait and choose our behavior? The wait can be a few seconds needed to decide on a response, to several days or more to choose the appropriate moment to get back to the other person or handle the situation. The wait gives us choice. Choice is freedom.

It is important to learn to avoid having our buttons pushed by others. "He who angers you controls you," the saying goes. You need to stay in control of your behavior. It may be important to learn to "hide" (not deny) our emotions when it serves us best. I think we have all learned to do that. We don't like to show fear or pain. That's why we get angry. But showing anger is not always to our advantage either. Having the choice of behavior, regardless of the event, is liberating. It is freedom.

Freedom to Decide on Action

So being aware of the emotion, labeling it, is that very important first step. Choosing our response, our reply, is the most important next step. Thinking about consequences is the way to decide what we are going to do. Do we let that other person push our buttons, and maybe cause us to embarrass ourselves with our behavior or get into trouble for being too aggressive? Or do we decide to choose our best path? Do we take the time to identify our best path? Do we use a Decision Tree?

You may be laughing, thinking you're not going to sit down and do a written exercise before you punch out that annoying guy. But you would probably be better off if you could. Also, when you are familiar with how to use the trees, you can do it very quickly in your head and get a glimpse of the likely consequences. In some ways, we all do that: it is automatic. We learn to calculate what is going to happen next. It does need to become automatic. We want to be able to choose our acts based on their consequences, not our impulses at the time.

Think about how a football coach uses strategy to attempt to control the game. The coach doesn't tell the players to run around the field in a free-for-all the entire game; it is much better to have a strategy that the other team doesn't anticipate. That helps in getting the desired outcome: winning the game. A free-for-all would leave too much to chance. More people would get hurt and it would likely be chaos.

You may be thinking that thinking about consequences is just too much work. But, you know we all do think about consequences, particularly when we are misbehaving. We often decide to lie to avoid negative consequences. We've all done it. That means we do know what consequences are; sometimes we just want to avoid them. Sometimes, we lie and it "works." That means the other person believes our lie. But not always. And there is the bigger problem: we know we have lied to or deceived others, often the people we love and respect. We know it is not a workable solution. We don't feel too good about ourselves. Sometimes, we feel really bad about the way we behaved. And we are still liable to get caught and get a worse consequence when the truth comes out (as it usually does). So, it's not a good strategy at all.

To avoid making such a poor choice, we need to decide ahead of time whether we want to suffer the consequences of that poor choice. We have a choice. We are free. We have what is called free will. We can decide for ourselves. If you attend religious services, you've heard it many times. Maybe you knew what it meant, maybe you didn't. Maybe, you didn't realize that you had that free will all the time, that you make decisions using that free will all day long. Tiny decisions, big decisions.

So, how do we sort things out for ourselves? How do we know what to decide? It seems so complicated. That is why it is so important to know ourselves, to know what we want for ourselves. If we let our inner voice and our thinking guide us toward our future, it is much easier to make good decisions, decisions that keep us on our way to our goals. Life becomes much simpler when we are in touch with our inner self. We are not "all over the place," making decisions that take us in many directions. Our life doesn't feel out of control. When we do not have a vision, a goal, a sense of ourselves, we feel lost, adrift. Life is difficult and out of control. My name for this book is about needing to know ourselves, who we are, who we want to become.

Some people believe that that inner voice is the voice of God guiding them to a good life. This voice gives them strength and conviction.

It is very empowering for them. We all have a sense of what is good for us. Deep down we all have a spiritual need to be in harmony with ourselves and with the world around us. But sometimes our anger or despair seems to silence that voice. However, in those moments, it is essential to seek it out, to hear it again, and to listen to its wisdom as it can save us from negative decisions and behaviors.

Getting in touch with yourself, with that inner voice, and being aware of who you are and what you want for yourself, becomes essential. That is the work of adolescence. If you are lucky, you have already learned to be in charge of yourself and managing your behavior when you enter that second decade. You have a head start toward managing your life. Still, as you become more independent during your teen years and beyond, you need to develop that into awareness and make choices to move you along a good path for yourself.

Don't think that this is easy or quick. It is a process that takes years and even continues throughout our adult life. We always have to make choices and decisions as to what we need, what is best for us, what the consequences are. No one knows the future, but we can use our wisdom to avoid pitfalls and poor consequences. We can do our best to position ourselves so that we "win." We can pay attention to ourselves and to the world around us.

 An easy example: The sky is cloudy. It might rain. Do we decide to take a coat or an umbrella, just in case? Or do we say: "I'll take my chances" and do just that? It may or may not rain on us later.

We have a choice. Can we take a moment to think about consequences? Where am I going? Whom will I be seeing? What if I walk in soaking wet? What kind of impression will that make? Do I care? Will it inconvenience someone else? What does it say about me? How do others see me?

You may be thinking that this is a stupid example. Old people take umbrellas. Young people don't care if they get wet. Or maybe, they believe it won't happen to them. Young people tend to think that they can get away with taking chances. Young people are more likely to be forgiven if they show up drenched. An older person might be thought of as foolish, not having much foresight. Not too smart.

Having foresight is certainly something that needs to be learned in adolescence. This is just another name for thinking about consequences when making choices.

◆ ◆ ◆

Let me share something that happened to me when I was about 19. I was on my way to an interview for a job as a part-time reporter for a small, local newspaper. The bus was slow in coming, so I decided to walk the couple of miles. It was a very windy day and I sort of enjoyed the walk. It took a long time and I just rushed into the interview instead of checking up on my looks in the bathroom beforehand... After the interview, I stopped at the restroom and saw to my great dismay that my face was totally covered in very visible dark dust (picked up by the wind). Needless to say, I never heard back from the newspaper. I have always felt very stupid about this mishap. You can see that thinking things through is important; not doing so can set you up for bad surprises and poor outcomes.

This example may seem foolish, even ridiculous. But think about it in terms of our understanding of the universe. We look at the sky. Do we not recognize low-hanging clouds, rain clouds? Do we not get signals from the world around us? Do we pay attention? Do we listen? The same needs to be said about the inner universe. Spirituality, listening to the inner voice, can be as simple as that. It is actually very simple and straight-forward.

Life doesn't have to be more difficult. It is often straight-forward once you follow your inner voice. Unfortunately, for many young people, it has been made complicated by the lives they have lived in early childhood. They are not sure where they stand, what their role is. Their families have been out of balance, living with many problems such as unemployment, drug abuse, illness, poverty; teens may have experienced multiple separations from parents and siblings, instability. It is not the children's fault. They are not responsible for their parents' distress.

It is important for these young people to understand that their own life can be very different. Often, these teens are angry, feel that life hasn't been fair to them. They are right. Their parents have gotten lost for many reasons, some of them their own, some because of the way things are, reasons that are too complicated to go into in this book. But the children still have a choice. They can get stuck in that anger and despair, or they can move beyond it and find ways to have a good life.

It is my biggest and most sincere hope that this book will help young people who are having a tough time figure out how to have a good life. It is my hope that the lessons in this book will be understood by even the most frustrated teens or young adults, and that they will serve as stepping stones toward more awareness of choice and empowerment to choose the life they want for themselves. You have choices, you always have choices.

You may remember that I first used the Identity Scale in a shelter with young people who were having a very hard time. They saw this new awareness as a way to cling to hope for themselves. They saw their ability to make choices, to have some control over their lives, as their ticket out of the hard times. They were right. It was their best hope.

Self-Soothing – the Magic that Helps You

Remember the story I told about Jason, the boy in the shelter many years ago, the one who learned to manage his anger and got the results he wanted – to speak to his cherished girlfriend in the hospital? Remember that before he could find better ways to get results, he had me listen to him and help him release his pain, his anger, his worry?

One of the most important things to learn in order to manage our behavior is what we call self-soothing. What do we do when we experience negative emotions such as anger, fear, or sadness? Even once we have chosen our response and it is adequate, we are often left with all those unpleasant feelings. They do not necessarily go away all that fast.

It is most important to learn how to take care of ourselves at that time. I have already mentioned the many ways we can be destructive when we try to drown out those painful feelings. We can act out in negative and dangerous ways. We can consume alcohol and use drugs, binge-eat, or sometimes cut ourselves to relieve the pain. We can become aggressive. We can engage in risk-taking, dangerous behaviors.

So, how do we find good, positive ways to take care of ourselves? First, we do need to acknowledge and face the feelings. We need to realize that the intense feelings will only last a few seconds or a minute, and then they will begin to dissipate, to fade. Of course, they can return repeatedly every time we think about certain incidents. It is important to let these difficult feelings be part of our experience. Let them flow over you. Remember the boy, Jason, who just "let it all hang out" before being able to move on.

Pushing the feelings down, what we call "repressing" them, is very harmful to us. As the saying goes: "holding on to anger is like drinking poison and expecting the other person to die." When we do that, those feelings erupt with a vengeance at the moments we least want them to. A bad temper and road rage are examples of repressed angry or hurt feelings surging up out of control.

The best way to release unpleasant feelings is to cry, scream, or yell. Unfortunately, our society disapproves of this but maybe you can find a space where you can release that frustration. After you have acknowledged the pain and hopefully been able to let it out, you can find safe ways to self-soothe by engaging in activities you enjoy. You can go for a walk, engage in sports, go meet friends or communicate with them through electronics and get their support. That last one is one of the best ways to get what you need: empathy and support. Some people also enjoy being alone, listening to music, reading. Being outdoors is often soothing. Nature is healing if you can have access to just a little patch of grass or a couple of trees. Some people like journaling, keeping a diary; writing about their experience; these can also be very helpful ways to cope and to learn from the experience.

 <u>Some examples:</u>

One of my young patients said that when he is angry or frustrated at home he goes out to run and usually ends up the street, climbing into a tree that he loves. Maybe he feels safer up there or maybe he feels he can see his path more clearly. I don't know. But I do know that he says it helps.

We all have favorite places where we go, sometimes to hide, sometimes to be left in peace, to "lick our wounds" and do some healing of our feelings, ourselves. When I was little, there wasn't really any place to go. My mother was always watching my sister and me very closely.

What I did was go into my mind. Many people do that. I just used to get busy separating myself from everything going on around me by thinking it through in my mind. I felt safe there. I felt I could be left alone while I worked on private things.

Some schools now have a space for students to go to when they are upset; they then are encouraged to sit still and be quiet, to practice mindfulness – taking care of themselves in the moment, thinking things through for themselves. This is wonderful and has proven to be very helpful to the students. They are able to calm down, engage in self-soothing, and regain their balance. Maybe, this is something we can do at home, or even at work, when we are older.

What do you do when you are upset? Do you cry, yell, or scream? Do you have a favorite place or a favorite activity? If you don't, it is important to find one. I didn't have access to music in my home. There was one record player (this was a long time ago) and I wasn't allowed to touch it. Nowadays everyone has their private way to listen to music. Do you have songs that you relate to?

One of my young clients once brought her CD player to her session and let me listen to the songs that she liked to hear when she was alone and hurting. She even danced to them. I felt so privileged to be trusted with something that was so important to her.

I am not sure what my children did. I didn't intrude. I do know that my daughter spent a lot of time on the phone. She often took care of friends who were distressed. I know she struggled a lot with her own difficulties but things got much better when she became a young adult.

My son, who lived with his very strict father, was often grounded at home. I don't know what he did to take care of himself. I guess he probably spent a lot of time playing video games. I think they seem to help many people. However, they do so by distracting from the pain, not by helping you deal with the pain. It is important to deal with the pain.

My son was later very unhappy during his twenties. I think he carried that anger from his teenage years when he couldn't find ways to heal from his anger. Distraction just delays the pain. It really made my son's life very difficult to have to deal with that delayed anger. He had a tough time in relationships and jobs until he learned to face the pain and confusion and make better choices for himself.

I will share what I do now when I am feeling emotional pain. Yes, having a strategy for this is something that is necessary throughout life, as there will always be some unpleasant or painful things. For small, everyday concerns, I go for a walk or I go for a swim – this always clears my head, as the water is very soothing. I also meditate for a few minutes just to find peace and calm, to let the stress just wash over me and then float away.

Often, like many others, I will also go to a place of worship where I can find peace and the chance to center myself and slowly heal. For larger problems, I do all the above things and sometimes I seek counseling if I can't sort it out by myself. Yes! Even psychologists need counseling sometimes—it is our duty to make sure we're in the best shape to help our clients. (If we're thinking about our own problems, it is hard to focus on clients and be helpful).

My daughter, who is now an adult, says that she takes deep breaths and walks in the sunshine: it always makes her feel better. Sunshine, or at least sun light, provides an essential vitamin that helps us function better. When I volunteered in the shelter, I took the teens out for walks or work in the garden. The air and the activity were both wonderful for them. They usually were much more peaceful when they came back in. It can help us all to spend time outside.

As I write this, I am remembering an 11-year-old boy who said he couldn't go outside to play with friends because it was too dangerous. Many others have also told me that, and I never know what to say. It is so painful to know that children are at risk in their own neighborhoods. Of course, something has to be done and is being done, but change does seem to come about very slowly. Later, I will talk about afterschool programs that are safe places and provide teens a chance to be at peace.

If you have read the many examples I just shared, you can see that there is an enormous difference between facing painful feelings, acknowledging them, finding ways to heal from our pain, and finding ways to avoid our feelings, distracting from them. When we write about our feelings, it helps heal the pain. Listening to music that speaks to our feelings is also healing. Playing video games or doing drugs, however, is a way to escape from those difficult feelings and does nothing to heal them. Sometimes, we become addicted and things just get worse from our lack of being able to manage and heal. We still have that work to do.

When people go into treatment for drug addiction, they are offered experiences that help them learn to face their problems and find ways to solve them. They are offered ways to help heal past hurt and build a life they can be happy with. It is very hard work, but it is work that is well worth doing. It is the work of life, your life if you need it. There will always be problems and uncomfortable and difficult things such as disappointments and losses. It is important, even essential, to learn how to manage those times. Doing so can give us a feeling of strength and control, a feeling of power that we can deal with tough things.

In the next chapter, I will help you see that as you grow in your teen and onto your young adult years, you essentially become your own parent. You are learning to be the one to manage your life. It is an exciting time as you see yourself growing in freedom and autonomy (managing yourself). It is a struggle, but it is your struggle toward having your best possible life. Think of the little child you once were, who struggled to learn to walk. As many times as you fell down, you got back up, determined to master what other people were doing. It seemed easy but it wasn't so easy for you. Yet, you were determined to do it, too. Once you mastered it, it did become easy. We walk without even thinking about it.

Now that you are a teen and soon entering adulthood, your life force is just as strong as when you were little: you can use it to your advantage. Be determined to walk and take your place in the world around you. Make it an exciting place for yourself.

Chapter 6

Parenting Yourself:
Learn to Be Your Own Guide

Dr. Françoise Dolto, a very fine French doctor who had a special understanding of how children and teens live their lives, often encouraged even very young children living in difficult conditions to parent themselves. She wrote about helping ten and eleven-year old boys whose fathers were absent, to become fathers to themselves. That means that she invited the youngsters to speak to themselves and guide themselves as they wished their father would speak to them and guide them.

 When I worked in the public schools, I once helped a seven-year-old boy whose father was in prison. This boy was very ashamed of his father and seemed to feel that this shame also included him. He was acting out in class and doing very poorly even though he had been a good student before his father had been arrested. I talked with this boy and helped him understand that his father's bad behavior wasn't his; he was not responsible as he had done nothing wrong. He didn't have

to be ashamed of himself. His father was paying for his bad behavior; that's how things work.

I then encouraged the boy to be his own father while his father was in prison. I told him that he could tell himself when he did well and reward himself with praise. He could also warn himself when he was tempted to behave badly. He clearly knew the difference. This boy took this to heart and immediately changed his behavior and became a successful student again, almost overnight. I only saw him twice; I did hear from his teacher how well he was doing. It seemed almost magical to the teacher.

But it wasn't magical. We can all take care of ourselves in that way. We can do it when we are sad and hurt and we can also do it when we feel good about ourselves and our world. We call that "listening to our inner voice."

I started this chapter with this story because I wanted to highlight it for two reasons. One is that it was just wonderful for this boy. At the age of seven, he knew right from wrong; he knew what would make him happier and he was willing to care for himself in a positive way. He no longer felt inclined to punish himself for his father's crime.

For most of us, our parents are the voices that guide us when we are very little. They take care of us and teach us what is good for us, what is bad for us, what behavior is acceptable, and what behavior is not. We learn to take their teachings into our head. We always hear their voices guiding us. This is normal. This is how we learn to take care of ourselves. Once we're in school, our teachers teach us much more than just Reading, Writing, and Math. Those are important subjects, of course, but learning the classroom rules, learning how to get along with others, how to play fair, to take turns, to respect others, to be honest about our experience, our learning – that's the most important.

Without these voices from others when we are little, we would feel lost. We wouldn't know how to behave in the world. What happened to the seven-year-old boy is that once his father became a "bad" person in his eyes, the boy lost his faith in his father. Since he identified with his father, since he felt he must be like his father, he no longer believed in himself either: he no longer believed that he could be good. This, also, is normal. We are "wired" to follow in our parents' footsteps. If we want to avoid that, we must become conscious (aware) of our choices. We do not have to follow in their footsteps if that is not good for us.

We can choose to parent ourselves as we wish to be parented, and choose our own paths separate from our parents.' How many times have we heard teens and young adults say: "I am not going to do what my mother or father did? I don't want to be stuck there." I know that I said that to myself and others many times. I often didn't approve of what my parents did or the way they handled things.

Each of us has the power, the freedom, and the responsibility to become our own parent. It is a normal part of growing toward adulthood. It is OK to be different from our parents, to make our own choices. It is OK to pick and choose what we want from what we learned from them, either through their words or their examples. That is the essential work of the teenage years.

This is our opportunity to make up for what's been missing. Some parents are absent, unavailable, too lenient, too strict, too trusting or not trusting enough, too demanding, or not expecting enough. Some are very kind and caring and some are unable to offer us that. It is very difficult to grow up with parents who do not treat us the way we need to be treated. Remember that no one is perfect and most parents who seem to fall short have pasts that cause them to fall short.

However, this doesn't need to limit us and our chances for a good life. As a matter of fact, it must not limit us from having the lives that we want. It is up to us to make up for what's missing as we begin to take over our own parenting, establish our own direction. This is possible at whatever age you are. It was possible for the seven-year-old with the father in jail. It is a hard road for many, but it is the only one if you want to attain a good life for yourself. If our parents were limited by their past, it is because they didn't know how to find their way forward. It is sad for them and for us. But, once we are aware, we realize that we have a choice and we have different possibilities: it is our responsibility to choose for ourselves.

So, how do we make up for what they weren't able to provide for us? Some parents are too busy with their own goals and ambitions. Some parents are depressed and often using alcohol or drugs and therefore not able to parent us the way we need. Some parents have to work too hard to support their families to have much time or strength to help their young ones. Some parents are angry and mean in the way they take care of us. Some parents are even abusive verbally or physically. Sometimes, parents are very immature and unthinking: they even abuse their children sexually, which does extreme damage to them.

Of course, when there is abuse in the family, it is essential for you to seek help outside of the family. There are counselors at school and other people in the community who can help you. There are agencies created to take care of children and protect them. It is your responsibility to let it be known that you need the help. Sometimes, this seems very scary, but most often it is the easiest way out of pain and toward a better future.

Most of your parents' shortcomings are not illegal or criminal, however; there is often no direct intervention available like with abuse. There is help, though, and it is up to you to seek it when you are depressed and discouraged, or frustrated and angry. I talk more about this in other chapters. The essential thing is to know you are not alone and adults are there to help you along the way.

So, what if your parents are not the way you need them to be? Can you become your own parent, guiding yourself through life? Can you encourage yourself when you are afraid? Can you soothe yourself when you are hurting? Can you give yourself credit and praise yourself when you put up a good effort? Can you warn yourself when you want to do something you know is wrong? Can you forgive yourself your mistakes? Can you learn to do all these things for yourself? If so, then you have become your own parent, at whatever age you are now.

These things are what our parents usually do for us but we must take over those tasks and become our own parents as we grow through the teen years and into adulthood. This is important even if our parents have been attentive to us as children. One day, we must take care of ourselves independently. Soon enough, we'll be taking care of others who need to learn those skills from us: our children!

◆ ◆ ◆

As I mentioned earlier, some people have a strong religious faith and God is the parent for them, guiding them on the straight path. Then it is easy for them to find and hear the voice. It is God's, but it is also theirs to listen to. What if you don't have a faith? What if you can't hear the voice? What if the voice you hear is mean and out to defeat you? Even if you don't have a strong faith, you can hear that voice inside you that is striving for your healthy survival, for your success. Everyone has it. It is instinctual to want to live and to succeed. It is our birthright. It is our birthright to want to make our lives the best and ourselves the strongest that we can be.

Sometimes, your helpful inner voice has been drowned out by the mean voice of your parents and others who were angry. You probably grew up thinking that they were angry with you, that you deserved it. You didn't know any better. No one deserves an angry voice telling them that they aren't good, that they won't amount to anything.

When that is the voice that you've been hearing, that voice needs to be quieted down. It was your parents' but their anger had nothing to do with you. Their anger was about them and things in their life.

The mean voice must be quieted down. It isn't yours at all. Once you can quiet it down by reminding yourself that you don't deserve that voice, you can start hearing the good voice, the voice caring for you. It has been trying to get heard. I think sometimes you did hear it when you told yourself: "it isn't fair." You knew you wanted better treatment for yourself, a much better life. That's the voice to listen to. Remember, everyone deserves a good life.

 I am going to share something of my personal story again. It is difficult for me, as it still hurts. My father was a bit of a bully. He didn't like it when I spoke up, when I disagreed with him. Once, when I was about nine years old, he got angry and told me that I was stubborn and that no man would ever love me if I behaved like that.

That bad voice stayed with me for a very long time and I am old as I write this book. I did quiet it down, many times. I had to remind myself that a good man doesn't want a doormat for a wife. But in my relationships, I found it very difficult to be assertive, to speak my mind honestly. I learned at an early age that I had better go along with men. Having to go along with the man was so ingrained in me.

Yet, I am not alone. Many generations of women were brought up to submit to a man's authority. That has led to many abusive and unhappy marriages. No one should have power over another human being. I work with many women who suffer because they feel their life is not really their own. They have had to fit in with others' expectations and there was no room for them. Does that mean that you have no chance to do better because many of us have struggled with it for so long? No, not at all. With this book, you already have a head start on me! Your generation can be much nearer to a healthy equality between men and women.

I'd like to stop here and talk about having power over children. This is somewhat more complicated. Our job as parents is to provide for children, protect them, and help them grow up into healthy beings. Yes, we must teach them to obey rules and we are responsible for punishing them for not following rules that help them fit in the world. But having power over anyone, including children, can lead to abusing that power.

Many children are abused, are terrified of the adults around them who wield a very unhealthy power, mostly through verbal and physical violence. Often, these children learn that violence is power and they go on to become violent with others in order to get their way. This is, of course, very unhealthy for them as well as for their victims when the destructive behaviors are repeated over and over again.

So, isn't there hope for change? My answer is that there just has to be. We want a better life for ourselves in a better world. If so, we must become the agents of change for ourselves and others. Remember, sometimes it takes more than one generation. Still, any good you do for yourself will help others as well. So, it is important not to let yourself be discouraged by rough or tough beginnings.

We all know what it feels like to be treated unfairly, to be mistreated; some of us have been victims of violence. Being told that no one will like you because of the way you are…is verbal abuse. We must not accept this voice, the mean voice, the one that treats us poorly. Sometimes, it can feel very hard to reject all these bad voices and find the good one. We may feel we don't have a good voice. But it is always there. I guarantee it. It is the voice that wants us to survive, to live a good life, to succeed.

So, give yourself a chance. You would give someone else a chance. You would even give an animal a chance. Some of us are kinder with others and with animals than we are with ourselves. Let's learn to give ourselves that kindness. Become your own good parent, your kind parent, the one who recognizes your struggle, your efforts, your successes, your defeats. Be your own parent who will see the good in you, who will hold you up when you feel weak or hurt, who will salute you when you feel strong, and who will remind you when you go off in the wrong direction. Be your own good parent who will keep you on the path to your goals.

But it is not enough to become your own good parent to guide yourself to a better life. In addition to being your own good parent, you need to seek that kind of uplifting support from your friends. This means finding good friends who are kind to you, who have your best interest at heart, who support you. At the same time, you can learn to be that kind of friend to others.

You already know how you feel when you are around people who are abusive, who are not good for you: you know what you don't want to have in people you welcome into your life. Learning how to recognize and then avoid those people who do not have good intentions toward you is essential. In turn, learning how to find and choose those friends that are good and supportive is extremely important. It is so important that it is discussed in many places throughout this book.

Chapter 7

Enlist Needed Help:
You Are Not Alone

In the last chapter, you read how I encourage you to be your own parent in order to guide yourself through life. This is something everyone has to learn: we do become our own guides throughout our lives. You have your teen years to learn how to *begin* guiding yourself and your lifetime to master it. While this is a basic and essential skill, it is most important to remember that you are certainly not alone in trying to master it. You are not learning to live all by yourself in this world.

At the end of the last chapter, I wrote about picking friends who support you and help you become the best you can be. The world is very crowded. There are plenty of people out there who can help. As a matter of fact, our world is set up so that children, teens, and young adults are guided in their lives. Home, school, and community all offer help in teaching and guiding them toward independence.

I began this chapter with saying that you are not doing this alone. Maybe you know John Donne's poem in which he states that "no man is an island unto himself." So, no one is alone, even if it seems pretty lonely sometimes. As a matter of fact, none of us could make it entirely alone, without all those people teaching us how to be in the world. Even Robinson Crusoe who survived alone on an island (in a story by Daniel Defoe) had already learned all kinds of skills for survival before he became stranded.

Fortunately, none of us is stranded alone on an island, as in Defoe's story. We are very much surrounded and supported in our lives, even if sometimes it doesn't feel that way. That help is essential. It would be hard to imagine not having the basic help we need to survive. We have people who grow and prepare our food, make our cars, make our electronics. There are medical people who help us when we are not well. The world is full of interactions between people. We may all resent having to go to school every day, but there is just so much to learn for us to be able to understand and manage our lives and find our place in the world.

As we strive to become independent and self-sufficient, we all need all the help we can get. This may sound contradictory, but it is not. We need to learn the skills we will use in the world. We learn them from others who teach us. Basic skills are still learned at home. How to manage our personal cleanliness and daily welfare: getting enough sleep, preparing and eating meals, grooming and dressing appropriately to go to school or out in the community. We also constantly engage in learning to manage relationships in the family, to answer to each other, to accept responsibility for our choices, to manage chores, to succeed in endeavors, school, sports, and community activities, and sometimes jobs.

What we learn at home, we then take into the community: the way we present ourselves to others, the way we tackle problems with our school learning, challenges to our physical abilities, or interpersonal difficulties. What we learn at home determines whether we solve problems with our skills or with force. This is mostly true when we are very young. As we learn to guide ourselves, to choose the way we want to be with others, it becomes our choice.

It is important to learn as much as we can so that we have the skills to succeed. None of us is born knowing the skills that we learn in school, such as writing and math; none of us is born knowing how to manage among others. These are skills we are taught by those around us.

As you struggle to grow through this decade and beyond, going from being a child managed by your parents to an independent adult, it becomes more and more your responsibility to gather the help you need to get you where you want to go. Home is not always providing the help and the skills that you need to learn. If you don't get the needed teaching at home, school can be more of a challenge.

For example, many children come to school already knowing how to manage well in the classroom and with other children, but many others still have to learn how to behave with classmates as they begin school. This is challenging and the children often feel at a disadvantage from the beginning. However, it is only the beginning of their education and they will have many occasions to learn those skills. Most children manage to overcome this early obstacle and make good progress in school.

You are in school to learn, and that knowledge is your due. Remember that teachers are always there to teach you. They want to help you acquire knowledge and skills, but it is up to you to learn and to let them know when you are feeling challenged, when you need extra help. We all need help at times; it is entirely normal. Also, it is important to ask for help because, if you wait till they notice you are doing poorly, you are already much further behind. So, it is your responsibility to ask for help in class or outside of class.

You can get help with skills from your teacher in the classroom, but also before and after school, if you need it. Don't forget that it is your job to go and get it. If you are hungry and need more food, you don't wait till someone thinks of offering it to you: you ask for it to make sure that you get it. In this world, we have to "look out for number one." You've heard that expression. It is true for everyone.

If your school doesn't offer enough help, you can find after-school programs that can help. You can even go online to see the lessons again. Many school districts have the school work online for just that purpose. You can ask your parents to help you with this. For high school students, there are programs that teach skills. They are often free and open to anyone. A very good one is Khan Academy, which offers free lessons on everything you need to know in High School and some college, too. There is also a lot of information on YouTube, but you may have to search a bit for what you need. However, today teens are much better at finding things on the internet than many adults.

You can go to your school counselor and find out what is available to you. Counselors are there to help you with your needs. They are there to guide you with community resources and are also there to help if you are having personal problems. Often, a teacher will notice that you're having a tough time and will send you to the counselor for help. However, here again, it is better not to wait till others notice – just go as soon as you need help. When life is hard, there is nothing wrong with getting help to make it easier.

I want to point out again how important it is for you to take charge of getting the help you need. When you were younger, your parents took care of attending to what you needed. But as you grow older, there are two issues to think about. The first issue is that your parents may not know what is going on with you. They may or may not be paying attention to how you are doing. Often, teens hide from their parents what is going on with them. It is normal to want your privacy and not let your parents know what is happening to you, whatever your reasons. Therefore, it becomes your responsibility to become aware of your needs and to begin to attend to them.

So many times, I hear from young people: it's too embarrassing to ask for help in the classroom or to go to an afternoon tutorial. Remember: it is the teacher's job to help all the students. Yes, it is difficult to ask for help, but you need to decide whether you are worth it. I hope you'll decide that you and your dreams are worth getting the help you need. It is there for you to get it. But, you know the saying, you can lead a horse to water, but you can't make him drink. Therefore, you have to help yourself.

The other issue is that, even if you share your problems with your parents, hopefully, by now, you will have realized that it is your turn to do something to help yourself. Of course, they will be there to help and support you. If it is a really serious problem, they will most likely take charge of getting you the help needed. But most problems can now be the responsibility of the teen to take care of. It is up to the teen whether he seeks a school counselor or not, whether she goes to an after-school tutorial to catch up on math problems she just can't get done. And don't give up! If one thing doesn't help, look further! This is the most important skill that you can learn in life!

Many times, parents and families are not aware of available resources. In high school and college, those things are usually said to you, not to your parents. This tells you that it is up to you to take care of yourself. In grade school, there are parent-teacher conferences, parent nights to show parents what their children are doing in school. All that disappears as you get older. You probably wouldn't want your parents to show up at school. They usually do so only when there is a major problem that you need help with.

So, let's look at who does what job in the high school. (We'll look at help beyond high school later in this chapter). You need to know whom to go to with your needs. Teachers plan lessons, teach classes, correct work, assign grades. Often, they also see students who need help either before school, during lunch, or after school. They can offer everyday help: that is how to keep up with the classroom work.

If a student has more difficulty, it is the teacher's job to refer the student to be evaluated for special educational help. The student's difficulties are then assessed and services offered to help with catching up or keeping up. Every student gets a personalized plan to help solve problems. It is very important to take advantage of whatever help is offered.

I will acknowledge here that there is often a stigma (a stigma is a negative attitude or judgment from others) attached to that kind of help. People don't want to be seen as different, weak, and needing help. You may be afraid that you will be sent to classes for "special needs" students. That is not necessarily true. There are many levels of help provided, and many of these are invisible to other students. No one else needs to know. For example, you may get special help on tests, like more time, or a different format. The important piece here, again, is not to let your prejudice keep you from getting what you need.

The school counselor helps with all kinds of difficulties that a student can have, beyond academic difficulties. (The guidance counselor is the one who helps with course planning and those very important college applications). Counselors are trained to listen to personal problems and help students: they can lead groups of students to help them improve their social skills, such as overcoming shyness; they provide some individual counseling; they can get help in case a student is being hurt or hurting others. A counselor can listen to whatever the student is going through, like having a parent lose a job, having an uncomfortable home where people fight, having someone close die.

The school counselor is also the one who knows about what help could be available to you in the community. School counselors can guide you to places that will meet your needs. Of course, it will then be up to you to follow through. In high school, people don't "hold your hand" like they did in elementary and middle school. You are considered responsible for yourself. This can feel very good even if it seems scary at times. You learn to do the things that you need to become an adult.

The school counselor can also refer you to the school psychologist. This person is trained to help with more serious personal problems such as depression, severe anxiety, anger, suicidal thoughts, or having experienced some trauma. Psychologists can help you sort through your problems and help you develop good coping skills, so you no longer experience these difficulties. The psychologist often speaks in classes and assemblies and teaches students to recognize that they're having problems that need help. Often, young people know that they are unhappy, but they don't know what to do about it. They don't know that there is help and that they can get better.

This is very important. Remember that you are not alone. There is help and it is just waiting for you to ask for it. There is no shame at all in seeking help with personal problems. It doesn't mean that you're crazy or weak. On the contrary, seeking help means that you are taking responsibility for yourself, for your future, for your happiness. You don't have to live with unhappiness or, worse, despair. Again, this is a difficult step sometimes, but it is a big step that will bring you rewards in many ways. It is a step you'll be thrilled you took—it will be very important on your path to your future.

S0, there is help in the schools. But there is help in the community as well. Often, you'll hear about it from school. You will be told to go somewhere and talk to people, sign up. You may want to talk to your friends and find out if they go to any of these programs. If they do, it's easier to find out about them and even to go there with them. If they don't, it is harder. You will be the pioneer to try things out. Friends may want to tag along once you start things rolling; you can then help others, be the leader they need. Sometimes, those community programs are offered in the schools as well, after the end of the school day. This makes it easier to get to; this helps teens avoid getting distracted or discouraged. A very good program that is present in many states is *Communities in Schools*; it provides very thorough and efficient help to students at risk of dropping out of high school, by drawing on community resources to furnish the needed help. If you can, go to their website (www.communitiesinschools.org) and read the many stories that are shared, especially *Jamal's story*.

Don't hesitate to be the pioneer in getting needed help! You can become the leader. It's a great role, even if it takes courage. Courage is a good thing. You needed courage to let go of the furniture and take that first step when you learned to walk. You needed courage when you went down stairs for the first time. You had the courage to do it. You moved forward. We all have had the courage necessary to get to where we are. I am sure you have enough courage, even if you feel scared and think that you don't have the courage. Courage means doing things that we fear. Courage is necessary to get you where you want to go.

Often teens test each other about their level of courage to do things that are a little risky or maybe outright dangerous. Some teens don't even hesitate to do those things. Though, I hope you would hesitate wisely when it is something dangerous that could harm your future, like doing drugs or trying some dangerous stunt. Everyone has courage. I challenge you to use some of that courage to do things that might appear unpopular, even nerdy, like getting help to succeed in school.

So, if you're told about community programs that help students with school challenges, or even programs that help with personal, emotional problems, please consider your need to succeed in life. I hope your need will be greater than your embarrassment or your shyness. These programs are there for people just like you and you certainly won't be alone.

Why should you need extra help? Why should you be behind or need to catch up? Sometimes teens are upset and angry when they feel that they are not moving as fast as others. This is difficult because it is rarely the teen's fault. Teens have experienced all kinds of lives and not all come to school work with the same preparation and aptitude. Some entered kindergarten already knowing how to read; many don't have that head start. Some children have a lot of support from their family for their school work, while other families don't have a space for their children to work peacefully. There are so many differences. It may not seem fair.

This, of course, is not your fault, but it is still your responsibility to catch up and keep up. The reason for this is that no one can do it for you. This is the absolute truth. In that way, unlike what it says in John Donne's poem, each person" *is* an island unto [him or her] self" and we each must take care of our own needs. The important piece is that even if you are behind, there are ways for you to catch up and have good opportunities in life. That part is entirely up to you and it is always possible, even if you have already dropped out of school. Think of Jamal's challenges (on the Communities in Schools' website) and his desire to overcome them.

An ideal home is one where the children had all the support and guidance that they needed to grow up easily. However, there is no such thing as an ideal home. A lot of time, there is little time and energy for support and guidance with one or two parents who work full-time. There are other children in the home. Sometimes, one or both parents are absent; there is instability, a lot of moves and changes of schools, and never enough time to keep up with the demands of school.

Sometimes, a child has attention deficit or hyperactivity, learning challenges and physical disabilities. These are challenges that make it even more difficult to study and be successful. I said more difficult but certainly not impossible. There are supports and help in the schools to help young people adjust to and manage the demands of school.

It's important to understand that none of these handicaps has anything to do with ability and intelligence. Let me repeat this most important fact: None of these handicaps has anything to do with ability or intelligence. That's most important. These problems do not take away from your being smart; you are still you, and you can meet challenges as well as anybody else. Children often consider others or even themselves to be dumb if they need extra services.

That's certainly not true! On the contrary, you are smart to get that help and you can count on your own smarts or intelligence to help you cope with these challenges. People with learning challenges often have higher than average intelligence. Did you know that Justin Timberlake, Will Smith, and many other actors, have battled challenges like Dyslexia and ADHD, their whole lives: they didn't let these challenges get in the way of their success!

Years ago, I had a blind friend who was in college with me. He had found ways to manage really well. He often got other students to read him from his textbooks in exchange for tutoring them in the course. He was great at concentrating: he knew he had to get it the first time he heard it, as he would likely not get a second reading... so, he was a great student who could help others, even though he was the "handicapped" one!

I just read about a blind musician who learns to play by ear. He listens to the music over and over again and then figures out how to play it. He has to figure out the chords and everything. He has trained himself to really focus on the strengths he has to make up for what he is missing. His main strength is to be smart enough to figure things out.

I want to add that once you accept your limitations, they become part of who you are and not a handicap. They kind of disappear as you compensate – find other ways – to get to your goals. I once had a friend who had lost a leg in an accident when she was very little and had grown up with an artificial leg since then. She never talked about it and probably didn't think about it either. No one knew about it unless she told them. She has had four children that she has raised with her husband of many, many years. She has a great career as a writer and teacher. Of, course, she doesn't ski or participate in sports, but she has a good life with what she can do. She learned to incorporate her "handicap" very early in life and has learned to live with what she can do.

Just like the three people above and the more famous ones mentioned before, we all have the smarts to help ourselves find ways to succeed. We all need to learn to do what we can do and not focus on what we can't do. What these people have in common is the will to accept themselves the way they are and to make the best of things. Making the best of it means having the best lives that they can have. We can all choose to do that. It is the most useful quality to have: it will get you the furthest in the world.

Unfortunately, many teens don't have the feeling that they can improve their lives. They feel discouraged. They don't see how they can overcome whatever has gotten in their way. They look around and see others who have given up. Yes, sadly, there are many adults who have given up. Sometimes, they haven't learned that they can find solutions. They have trouble understanding that it is really up to them. It is up to them whether they will give up or keep trying.

Sometimes, teens and young adults feel this way because they see others around them feeling the same. Or maybe they've been told or shown that there is no way out of a difficult life and that success is not for them or people like them. This is very sad, as success is for anyone who goes after it. Success doesn't mean that you become the best in the whole world at something; success means that you do what you want to do and feel satisfied with the way you lead your life. That kind of success can come to anyone who keeps his dreams and goals in mind.

Sometimes, teens or young adults feel it is too late. They have already gotten off the path. They have made mistakes that they think are beyond repair. This is very seldom true. It is important to realize and to believe that there is always a path open to you. The biggest mistake is to give up on what you would want for yourself. If you have messed with drugs or alcohol, it can certainly be serious, but it is up to you to get out of that and back on the path to your goals. Plenty of others have done it. You can do it, too.

Even if you have gotten into the justice system for whatever reason, the future is not closed off to you. Juvenile records get closed. Even if they don't, you can get yourself straightened out if you go get the help you need. Let me repeat it: go get the help you need. Sometimes, the help will come to you, but a lot of time, it is really up to you to go after what you need. Get information: it is out there. Keep your eyes on what you need.

 Some years ago, I worked with teens that were on probation and, most fortunately for them, were forced to go to group therapy once a week. Yes, they hated the idea. They were scared. They felt ashamed of

being on probation and having to face up to what they had done. They didn't realize at first that they were the lucky ones. They didn't go to jail. They were offered help. Some of the teens remained resentful and silent for a very long time. They were there but didn't participate in the group. Other teens warmed up to the counselors after a few sessions and made the effort to be present, to face up to their mistakes. They talked about their lives. They listened to each other talk about their shame, their sadness, their fear of the present and the future. Most of these teens had had difficult lives. Those who agreed to engage did much better than those who were unable to take advantage of the therapy. Some found not only their courage but also their hope for themselves, their hope for their future. It was very exciting to see some teens make plans to get their GED, maybe try for a trade school, or even a junior college to start. They now had ambitions for their lives!

People often give special honors to those who have recovered from a difficult episode. The recovered drug user who succeeds stands taller than a person who never had difficulties in his life. This tells you that effort is honored. It also tells you that overcoming such challenges really does happen... you can be the person who makes it happen to you. Why not? You are just as good as the next person. You can exercise your strength to make success happen. It is up to you.

So, how to keep your eyes on the prize when you live in difficult circumstances? Teens sometimes run into problems because they are unhappy with the way their life is going. They are unhappy at home. They feel it is not a good place for them. Their needs aren't being met. They are angry and frustrated or, sometimes, depressed. Depression is scary because the depressed person feels that there is no hope for things to change.

Let's look at why a teen is unhappy at home. Sometimes home is just not a good place to be. That is very painful. Parents may be too busy to give their children the attention and presence they need. Parents may be focusing on their own needs, leaving little time and energy for their children. Often, this is because they are working very hard to support the family. That's hard for children to understand. It is useful, though, if children know that their parents are having a hard time; then, they can relate to their parents' situation, and not take it so personally when their own needs are not being met.

Sometimes, there are other problems, some of them stemming from working too hard, or at jobs that are just not satisfying. Parents may be using alcohol and/or drugs to escape their unhappiness. This is a terrible situation for the teens because they are suffering from their parents' absence and sometimes violence due to drugs or alcohol; they are also shown that this can be a solution to their parents' problems, and maybe their own, too.

These parents often lose their jobs due to their use of alcohol and drugs. This makes things at home even worse. There are awful money pressures. There is more drug and alcohol use and more anger. Life at home can get very difficult. In addition, parents are often depressed about their situation and feeling hopeless to change it. Families fall apart. Often, a single parent has a series of partners. There are too many changes going on for anyone in the home to cope with. Children and teens are particularly sensitive to all these changes. These are very frightening. No one knows the future, but when these things happen, the feeling of fear, the fear of danger, is right there.

With all these pressures and the difficult example set by parents who give up and use, many teens do learn that this is an acceptable way to deal with frustration. They begin using. However, they need to realize that it doesn't have to be that way, that drugs and alcohol don't solve anything for their parents, that they can find their own, different, path to a better life. Remember, it is never too late to come to that decision. You can have been using drugs and alcohol, and then decide to find a better path, one that will lead you to success rather than misery.

Sometimes, before you can find and hang on to your dreams and goals, you need to get out of situations that are really bad for you. Sometimes, grown-ups are so caught up in their own problems that the home is outright toxic for the children. The children are left alone, unsupervised, and at risk of getting hurt. They are not fed and clothed as they need to be. Sometimes, they are left to wait alone in public places. All this is against the law. Children are often put at risk of physical or even sexual abuse from adults, and sometimes from siblings and other relatives. It is very sad when this happens and, unfortunately, it happens too many times. Statistics say that one in four girls and one in five boys are sexually abused. We know that it is happening.

If you need help, do it for yourself, for your siblings, even if it is scary to be separated from your family. It is more important to be safe. You must know that there is help. You can always go to an adult at school or in the community. At school, you will be sent to a counselor. It is the counselor's duty to call agencies that help children who are being abused or neglected. Of course, it is scary to get help. You expect that the law will step in and you'll be removed from your home. You'll go to some place that you've never been. Sometimes, this is true. Usually, it is temporary; you'll be able to go back home after your parents take parenting courses and commit to taking better care of their children. Sometimes, it is a parent or relative who must leave the home.

 I once taught parents who had their children taken away from them and were now attending classes to get their children back. These classes were offered by the state in an effort to bring children back into their families as soon as it was safe to do so. Most parents had been surprised to find out that their parenting was not good enough, that their children were distressed. They were confused as they felt that they had done their best. They had done the best they could but they lacked the education to understand their children's needs. In these classes, they became willing students and learned how to manage their children better.

It is certainly very scary to experience all these changes. However, many children and youths manage to have the courage to speak up and complain, even when they are being threatened by adults. It is necessary for them to be safe and they sometimes need to take that responsibility in their hands. These children almost always end up doing much better than those who don't take their safety in their own hands. Remember: it is what you do for yourself that empowers you. Your life becomes better, even if it is still very difficult.

I have worked with many adults who had been abused as children or teens. They have suffered a lot and they come to see me when the pain remains too strong. Still, despite the pain, many of them have managed to make good lives for themselves. They have often been the one who took things in their own hands and got out of the situation, sometimes by reporting it to a trusted adult who helped stop the abuse, sometimes by leaving.

 A woman patient told me that she had tried to tell her mother about being abused, but her mother wasn't able to listen. She didn't take her daughter seriously. My patient, who proved to be an enterprising seven-year old, went to a neighbor to report the sexual and verbal abuse (most sexual abusers also abuse with words, threatening their victims so that they don't tell). This person did hear her. Thank God. She shared with my patient's mother what she had heard and the abuse was then ended. Thank God, my patient had had the courage to get help. She knew it wasn't her fault and it wasn't right. Most children know that it isn't right but they don't always know that it is not their fault. However, it is never their fault, even if they are flirtatious teens. It is the responsibility of the adult to keep clear boundaries and not abuse the child's innocence.

Many patients, like the one in the example, have taken charge of their life and they have had the strength to move on, despite their fears and despite the pain. So, that is available for all of us. We learn to do whatever it takes to get ourselves to a good place. Fortunately, there is help: you don't have to do it alone. Remember that there are people everywhere who can help, whether they be relatives or neighbors, or people at church. At school, there are counselors and psychologists. In difficult times, you can even call the police if you are frightened. They are trained to help.

 When I was a psychologist in the schools a twelve-year-old girl came to talk to me. She reported that her parents beat her and all her brothers and sisters, and they were terrified. She was afraid to go home once she had told me. My duty was, and still is, to make sure she was protected. I called the police and made the report. The family was called in and the abuse report verified. This girl was quite brave: she even confronted her parents. All the children were immediately removed from the home and put in a safe place, a shelter. The parents were mandated to receive education and then have supervised visits with their children. I do not know if they succeeded in getting their children back or not, but I do know that the state does its best to protect the children if there are any concerns.

You can go to others in the community, youth counselors, church people, sometimes relatives and friends. They will call Child

Protective Services to help you, or even the police, if needed. A social worker will come and speak to you and then to your parents. They will do their best to help resolve the situation. It may be that you'll be placed for a short while in a shelter or group home so that CPS can help your parents learn how to take care better care of you. Your parents may have to take certain courses to satisfy CPS requirements. Sometimes, parents are not up to it and you'll end up in the foster care system. This is challenging, but most foster care parents are very good people who truly care about children in their charge. There, you'll have a chance to learn those skills that you may be behind in. You can use this time to catch up and get on a good path to your future.

Many children have been able to gain from foster care. They went into a stable family where children were properly taken care of. They learned to take better care of themselves and to make good decisions for their lives. I have worked with children and with adults who, as children, had lived with foster parents. They considered those new parents as much their parents as the ones they were born to.

Many people have heard horror stories about foster care and government agencies. They may be as scared of this "help" as they are of the abuse. But *Law and Order, SVU* is a TV show that feeds on people's fears about government agencies and foster care; it is *not* the reality of foster care. Yes, it is scary to go live with another family and it is remotely possible that it won't work out for you, but you can always seek help for that, too. I have worked with wonderful foster parents who did everything they could to get kids back on the right track: gave them love and helped them develop confidence in themselves.

◆ ◆ ◆

There is help in the community and elsewhere for young adults, as well. As you reach your later teen years, you may be in college or working full-time. Maybe you are still at home, trying to find your place in the world. For most young adults, this is an exciting time of managing new challenges and building their strength and self-confidence, as they grow in independence and autonomy. But many also experience difficulties that they feel unable to overcome by themselves.

Remember: there is help for everyone. This is a good time to remember to get help as needed. You may find the tasks of becoming independent and responsible very challenging, often due to delays caused by a difficult earlier life.

You may find it difficult to overcome the abusive voices that are still with you. You may be angry and turning to violence. Or you may have trouble setting clear limits (personal boundaries) with others in order to be treated well; you may lack assertiveness (being clear and direct with your words) to let others know your needs.

Some young adults engage in destructive behaviors such as drug and alcohol use; they and others are often anxious and depressed, due to their fear of failing in their development. Some young adults have difficulties finding a direction for their future. It is then high time to get the help necessary for you to grow into a successful adult. Remember that it is now your responsibility to get the help you need. Remember also that it is never too late to take good care of yourself.

If you are in college, there are counseling centers with many resources to assist you with your challenges. These services are included in your tuition and available while you are a student. If you are working full-time, employers offer Employee Assistance Programs that are free to employees. Your work place may also have additional resources for Well Health. Employers also provide health insurance to their employees; Counseling or Behavioral Health Services are most often available to help you cope with emotional problems and substance abuse. You can also find help for the different kinds of situations you may be experiencing by searching online for help you need.

If you are not working, there are public services for Mental Health and there is insurance through Medicaid and other programs. If you are disabled, Medicare covers this kind of assistance. Social welfare agencies can also help you locate the help you need. There are also clinics and there are always hot-lines and emergency rooms when you are in crisis. There is help everywhere you look and you can get what you need!

So, the gist of this chapter is that you're not alone, whatever your age or your need. There is always help available, whether your problem is small or large. It is up to you to take any help offered to you and to seek help when it is not offered directly to you. No one needs to feel alone or that they need to give up on a good life. We are all entitled to a good life. It is up to us to keep seeking it. Keep your eyes on the prize…it is yours for the taking.

Chapter 8

Identify Your Wishes:
Follow Your Dreams

In the last chapters, you've been learning how to manage yourself, your emotions, your behavior, your need for help. Now it's time to manage your dreams. Everyone has dreams. Maybe only one, maybe several. Dreams are important. They are essential. They give us energy and direction. To reach our dreams, we need to identify goals. Healthy humans are always reaching toward a goal. Sometimes, it's a tiny, daily goal: getting your homework done, spending time with friends, practicing a sport, scoring a goal or a basket, even getting your chores done.

But here we'll be learning about big dreams. Big dreams that guide your life. Dreams give life meaning and direction. Dreams are what we can't live without. Even if you feel that you don't have dreams, that life is just too tough and dreams don't come true anyway, somewhere deep within you, you have a dream. You may have hidden it carefully. You may be afraid that it's just a dream. You fear that it's impossible; it's never going to happen. Well, you can't be the judge of that. You never know what is possible. So, let yourself dream. And try to reach for that dream. Many people have succeeded despite very difficult odds. You won't know until you try.

Stevie Wonder became blind shortly after birth but went on to become one of the greatest jazz musicians! Dr. Stephen Hawking is today's greatest physicist even though he is completely paralyzed, able to type on a computer by moving only one finger almost invisibly! President Roosevelt governed this country from his wheelchair, resolving the employment problem of the Great Depression and leading the Allies to win World War II! He was president for four running terms! These are extreme examples of success but think how easily it could have gone the other way. They could have given up when faced with such challenges. But they didn't, they strove for a dream, their dream, they valued their chance at a good life for themselves and were determined to make the best with what they had. What victories! You can win, too!

If you want to succeed, you need to make your dream your guiding light, that which you are always striving for. You need to believe in your dream. Most people have doubts. That's normal. Still, they want to strive toward their dream. Have faith that your dream is right for you and work toward what is needed. Having faith in yourself and your strength to keep trying is essential.

Some people believe it is God's purpose for them. They want to remain faithful to their goals. It gives them a special strength and faith in being able to follow their purpose. It gives them the strength to accept frustrations and even defeats, the strength to keep going, striving toward their purpose, their dream.

On the other hand, some people feel that they just can't believe in dreams. So, what if you don't really believe in dreams? What if you think dreams are for kids, for dreamers? What if you don't feel entitled to dreaming: you've been told over and over again not to be a dreamer? Well, it can be really hard to find that dream that you had, or you may know just where you hid it in your heart in hopes of better days, a better time in your life. Maybe that time is now. It is never too early or too late to start on your path to your dream.

I know that many of you will likely dismiss this idea, but if I reach just one person and encourage them, I will be thrilled. Let that person be you. That would be so wonderful for you. Find a little faith in yourself and your dream. Give yourself a chance to see if you can find the strength to work toward a good future. There can be obstacles in your way – there always are – but don't give up. This chapter is about nurturing your dreams, feeding them, fanning the flames of your courage. Every day is an opportunity to move toward your dream. Little everyday steps are what build a future.

Since everyone has at least one dream, let's move forward and see how it is possible to achieve your dream. A dream doesn't become real until you make it happen. So, it is very important to start thinking about how to make it happen. Sometimes, a dream requires you to get more education either in school or in the community, as an apprentice. It is important to start setting goals to make the dream become a reality. It is most important to stay aware that the dream is the goal and that you need to create and walk the path to that goal.

It is important to share your dreams with adults and friends that you can TRUST to encourage and guide you. Many adults know about ways that you can get the help you need, and many are willing to help you get a volunteer or part-time job in the area you're interested to know more about. Say you want to be a fireman, then, hanging around the firehouse is important. Maybe you can volunteer to help. Don't expect to go out and attend to fires, but you can certainly get to know some of what it feels like to be a fireman.

Many youths have dreams about being a doctor, a nurse, or a lawyer. There are many opportunities for part-time and summer jobs to get to know about those fields. Many, many teens are interested in sports as a career. They generally know that they need as much training as possible. Most high schools prize sports and encourage their students to get involved.

Many teens have different dreams such as making money in business. Many have ideas what kind of business they want to enter. It is easy to work with people already engaged in those kinds of business. Even if it isn't a paying job, it is probably worth the education that you can get about how to run and manage a business.

Of course, there are after-school and community programs that help teens explore what they might want to do and choose dreams and goals. Many times, teens are not sure about their direction, so it is quite alright to start in one area and to change as you grow and find other things you might like. It is OK to switch many times. Our world is changing so fast that it is now unusual to do the same thing your whole adult life.

The most important thing is to never feel that you're not entitled to a dream, for whatever reason. Everyone is entitled to even lofty dreams. Everyone is given the opportunity to try. It is not always a straightforward path. Some teens who want to become doctors know they will go straight on to college and then try to get into medical school. But that's for some. Others know that they can't afford that direct a path.

But what would keep you from starting at the bottom, maybe getting a job with a high school diploma in a hospital? You'd be in the midst of the world you want to accede to. You may even get help with taking college classes and going for a college degree. Then, you can get into medical school from there. Or you could get into an associated field like nursing or working as a physician assistant and get yourself more experience. From there, you may decide this is good enough: after all, there are other important goals in life, such as having a family, taking care of children and other family members, etc. Or, you may still want to go to medical school and reach your original goal.

Many people find that they must adapt their goals to their current reality, so their goals may change over time. People make new and different decisions as they go along their own path. For example, when I was in high school, I wanted to do medical research. However, my father was very discouraging because my family was poor and he didn't think I had a chance. Neither he nor I knew that there were scholarships available and a lot of financial help was available to medical students.

It is most important to find out as much as possible about what is available. You find out from school counselors, college counselors, the web, the community, or people in your chosen career. It is so important to keep looking. I wish I had not accepted my father's negative verdict as the final word; I could have searched for more information.

My path: I had no clue when I was in high school that there were opportunities for help to go to Medical School. Like many of you, I had not grown up in this country, and my family didn't know about available resources. There was no Internet and we didn't know how to seek information. It is easier now, but it still has to be done. You have to take charge, to be in charge of your own life.

I went to college and followed another goal. Later, having finished college, I decided to go back to my old dream of going to Medical School and becoming a doctor. I took a bunch of courses and applied to medical school. However, in the meantime, I fell in love with the man who was to be my husband and decided to marry and stay at home with my children when they were little. Those were wonderful years. As my children grew up, my old dream started waking up again. But Medical school wasn't so attractive anymore, since I was getting older and didn't want such long work hours.

I had always been attracted to psychology and had done some very exciting reading in child and adolescent psychology during the last few years. This got me going and I decided to go back to school again and learn about psychology. I also volunteered in a shelter for adolescents to find out if that was really what I wanted to do. I loved working with the teens and felt I was right where I belonged. I eventually went on to do a doctorate in psychology (a Ph. D.) and have been enjoying this new career. It is a wonderful fit for me. I am able to help many people make a difference in their lives, and I also have time to do the writing and creating that is now becoming this book for teens and young adults. My hope is that this book will help them make a difference in their lives.

I shared my story to show you that there are many, many different ways to get where you're going. It is often good if you can change and adjust along the way. It is important to realize that one can change goals as one goes along, to find better or more fitting goals. In addition, it is never too late to be doing what you love, what you really want to do, what fits you best. It is so important to find that for yourself. It is the work, not only of the teenage years, but throughout one's whole life.

This week, I read in *Psychology Today Magazine* that students who come from poor or difficult backgrounds are more successful at meeting the challenges of college with aplomb (feeling sure of themselves) and momentum (keeping moving forward) than those who haven't had challenges to overcome. This is so because they have already learned to master difficulties and rely on their own strengths: students from richer families have had it much easier and often don't know how to manage obstacles. The poorer students may have to make up for academic work (classes) that they didn't take before, but they are better equipped for the real world than students who have not encountered challenges and difficulties before.

◆ ◆ ◆

Just a little earlier in this chapter, I suggested that you share your goals with people you trust, that you let others know your direction so that they can help you. But now, I need to say to be careful how you share your dreams. It is most important to protect your dream, to share it only when it is safe. What I mean is you need to share your dream with those who are not going to shoot it down, to deny you your dreams, to tell you "you're just a dreamer, get back to reality."

Those people are not really safe. Maybe you have the strength to get past their negative attitude and comments. Maybe you don't. I accepted my father's nixing my dream without even questioning it. Was I just stupid? No. I respected my father and assumed he must be right. I had no idea that he was wrong, that I could have gotten scholarships to study, etc. So, it is essential to take things with a grain of salt if you do share and get negative comments back. I must say that since then, all I need is to be told that something is impossible...and I jump into the challenge.

So, all I am saying is be careful to share with those who will encourage you, but be also ready to go your own way if you encounter negativity. Be sure to check your options out, to seek those who will encourage you. You may also need to soothe yourself, take care of yourself if you're hurt by negativity and maybe mockery from those you share your dreams with. Many people are negative because they gave up on their own dreams and are uncomfortable when others want to follow their dreams.

So, how to protect yourself and nourish your dream? How to take care of yourself if you're feeling hurt or discouraged? It is quite a challenge to shoulder your dream and decide to go on anyway. Some people thrive on the challenge; others take their time to lick their wounds. I know the times I felt discouraged just took the wind out of my sails. I chose another path or two. I moved forward kind of blindly. I did enjoy what I was doing at times, but I was not passionate about it. Yet, I found my path forward and my passion (love) for my goal again.

When you have a dream, a dream that really fits you, you are passionate about it, like I was instantly passionate about psychological studies, even when they were very hard. Some will tell you that it is unusual to be passionate about what you're doing, but it doesn't need to be. People who are really successful are successful because their passion gives them the energy to move past all obstacles.

So, even when you encounter negativity and discouragement, keep your eyes on the prize and decide to hold on to your dream with all your strength. I can't guarantee that you will make it happen, but I can tell you that you won't if you just let go of it. Being careful to nurture your dream privately is good, but overcoming others' negativity can also be good practice for a world that will often feel like it's getting in your way.

Following your dreams, striving toward your goals doesn't mean that it will always be a straight line from which you will never stray, or that it will be a difficult but direct path. No, on the contrary, it is rarely a straight path and you may get lost at times, take wrong turns, or have to backtrack and start again. Sometimes, you may even change goals, find new, unexplored paths. But it will be a journey, *your* journey. It is good to think of your whole life as a journey, a journey of twists and turns, gains and losses, ups and downs. Everyone's life is like that. It is never just a straight arrow from one end to the other. That's what makes life so interesting and challenging!

All I am saying is that it can be very good to have a direction of your choosing, as well as desires and goals for yourself and your life. Life can be a meandering river that adapts to the hills and valleys or it can be a rapid torrent that carves the landscape, choosing its own path as it barrels down. This may be a funny image, but there is something to it. If you have energy and direction, you are more likely to carve the path you need through your environment. If you just wander where your environment lets you go, you will have a very different life. The choice is entirely up to you. There is no right or wrong, just your preference, what fits you best.

Chapter 9

Keep Moving Towards Your Goals:
Avoid Being Distracted

This chapter is to show you what your life can look like if you decide to follow your dream intently. This applies to you, whether you are already committed to a dream, or you haven't decided what you want to do, or are not even sure you want to do the work of following a dream. It can certainly be intimidating or scary to commit to a dream. So, the first thing to do is to break it up into small steps, even tiny steps.

You need to identify goals and keep them in mind. If you want to go college, which is the necessary path to many dreams, you know that there are a lot of things to do to get into college. They start with tiny steps such as getting your homework done each day to get the grades that will move you forward. But it is not all just about grades. There is also the knowledge needed. People need to know a lot of things. Many times, students think that knowledge is unnecessary. I often hear "I'm never going to need to know about that!"

But that's not true! We all need to know a lot of things. Why? Because knowledge gives us a better understanding of the world. When we want to learn something, we watch how others do it. We copy them. This includes those who are no longer here, who may have lived centuries before us. They help give us a perspective, a view of where we are now, in our own time. Many people have lived before us and we are very lucky that, through books and writings, they shared their experience, how they did things. Their experience can often help us with all kinds of problems. We can also learn from their mistakes, what didn't work for them. Hopefully, if you aren't doing this already, you will begin to look at knowledge in this way. This will certainly help you thrive in your education and work. It will add passion to your studying and help you identify dreams and goals. There is so much that we still don't know. There is a lot of work to do. There's plenty of opportunity for everyone to jump in and contribute to knowledge in the world.

Let's say that your goal needs you to get a college education. You know that, for this, you will need to get good grades in high school and to graduate from high school. But what if you don't have good grades and don't get into college straight out of high school? What if you have already dropped out of high school? Well, it is certainly not too late for anything.

You can get a job while you work toward your GED. There is a lot of help to meet that challenge. There is help in the schools, in the community, on the Internet. You can even study on your own and get there all the same. Let's say you can't really afford college even if you can get in. There are scholarships. There are loans. You can also work and go to college part-time in person or on-line. Nowadays, there are just so many options that it is possible to find something that fits your needs. It can also wait till you're able to do it. No one is ever too old to go back to school. I was pretty old when I went back to school. I am even older now and I still have ambitions – like getting this book written and out into the world so that it can reach you and others it might help. I'm even going to write more books!

What if your goal doesn't include college? There are plenty of careers that need special schools but not college. You can work or get loans to attend these schools. There, too, it is important to put your whole heart in it and learn everything you can. That way, you will find an easier path to success in whatever you do. Maybe you don't think it is worth the effort. That's OK, too. It is just important to remember that the choice is entirely up to you.

Many times, people don't do well in school when they're young. They don't realize the value of succeeding. But remember that it is never too late. Sometimes, ten years later they realize that they're sorry they never went on with their studies but they still have a dream. Is it too late? Not at all! Remember, you can always make changes and move yourself toward the goal that you want for yourself.

 My daughter said I could use her story as an example here. She barely made it through high school. She was angry. She didn't want to go to college even though we, her parents, could offer it to her. She

practically ran away to get married to her boyfriend. He got into the Navy and she worked for a couple of years. She then got pregnant and had two little girls in two years. Then her marriage fell apart. For a while, she seemed lost.

Yet, she was very, very lucky. Her father offered to help her and the children if she went to college and maintained a good average. She jumped on the opportunity and applied to junior college, where she got a Pell grant and some loans to get by, in addition to her father's help. She worked harder than she had ever done. She succeeded in her courses. She soon became ambitious about having a good career and she was accepted in a four-year college. Spurred on by her success, she then chose to enter a Master's Program. She has just graduated, as I am finishing this book, ready to embrace her new career as—you guessed it—a psychotherapist!

Of course, few of us have that support (she still has a ton of loans to pay back, though), but it is important to take advantage of any opportunities, and to make changes that move you toward the goal you want for yourself.

You can move toward your goals in many ways. There is no right or wrong way. Whatever way works for you is the right way. Some teens and young adults want to get jobs as soon as possible and become independent from their families. Sometimes, they want a family of their own as soon as possible. Sometimes, they have already created a family without actually wanting to, but they want to make it work for themselves and their children.

That is a very noble goal. Accepting responsibility for what we do, whether we wished for the outcome or not, is the most adult thing we can do. It helps you become wise and careful in managing your future. Maybe you'll value an education more if you have to wait a long time before you can get it. Sometimes, people feel that they are preparing the way for their children. I talked about that earlier in the book. Sometimes, it takes a couple of generations to achieve lofty goals.

Whatever path you choose, it is most important to avoid getting distracted from it. There are always many events or people that will take us away from our path. It is unavoidable, but we still need to do what we can to avoid being thrown off the path. We must become very familiar with our goals and the path we have chosen. It is important to identify people and events that will move us closer and to avoid those that will push us away from our goals.

While we don't want to live alone in the world, we need to learn to choose friends carefully. Some teens like to have lots of friends but, as they grow toward adulthood, they'll learn the value of trustworthy friends, and will probably have a handful or fewer "real friends." We need friends who will honor our goals and encourage us when we feel weak; they'll remind us of our goals when we might go down the wrong path. Those are the friends who will help us become the persons we want to be. We need to be careful to avoid people who are jealous or destructive, who envy us and may wish for us to fail.

Sometimes, in romantic relationships, partners want us to be entirely devoted to them and their needs. This is not reasonable and it takes us away from our own goals. Sometimes, they want you to put all your energy into helping them toward their goals. Any relationship where your needs are not respected and honored is not a healthy relationship for you. A healthy relationship is where both partners are good for each other, take care to honor each other, and help the other meet their goals.

When we are with friends or romantic partners, we tend to get carried away by the feeling of closeness, and to trust that whatever happens is good for us. It is very tempting to feel that way. However, it is not always good for us. We have to make sure that our needs are understood and respected. That is not selfish -- whatever anyone else may tell you. It is totally necessary for your happiness and well-being. Furthermore, it is only when you take care of yourself that you can take good care of others and be truly generous, kind, and loving.

A very basic and important part of developing friendships is to see how well each partner has his or her needs met. In other words, is each partner truly happy and doing well within the relationship? Relationships grow or fail on that issue. Of course, it doesn't always have to be tit-for-tat or taking turns; sometimes one partner needs more support and the other can delay satisfying his or her own needs for a period, sometimes for some years in committed relationships, such as when one spouse works so that the other can go to college full-time.

But not forever. Partners must not give up their own goals altogether. If you are not taking care of your needs, you can become nasty, resentful, depressed, or outright angry with others, even if you like or love them. As said earlier, many relationships fail because the balance is not right: one or more of the partners is not getting his or her needs met.

One must always be on the lookout for one's safety and well-being. We deal with people all the time and this is the basic rule to determine whether they are good and safe people to be with. Not all people are honest and respectful of others. As a matter of fact, many people are manipulative, wanting you to fulfill their needs. They don't really care about you.

 I once worked for a long time with a pre-teen girl who liked to play with Barbie dolls. She would have them enact terrible ways of treating each other. There was usually a rivalry between two or three Barbie dolls fighting over Ken. They would deceive and trick each other or become partners to trick him into something or other. This was clearly the kind of unhealthy relationships that she was living with at home. It took some time to help her have the dolls be honest with each other and let each one be free to be who they were. It took quite a bit of time, a very long time. Unhealthy ways learned at home can have a strong influence on you, and it can take a lot of energy and time to change to more healthy behaviors for yourself. So, be patient! Don't give up!

Many people feel that others are there for their use, and they tend to use others to meet their needs. Of course, we all have needs that need to be met by other people but there are good and bad ways to get there. It is OK if we request that they meet our needs and then leave them the choice to do so or not. We inform them of what we want, but we must *not* impose on them that they have to satisfy our needs. An extreme example of imposing is bullying: "you must do what I want." Another, even more extreme example is sexual abuse: a healthy person respects others and their needs, but perpetrators overlook the needs of their victims.

Of course, teens and young adults are still learning how to be in the world. They make mistakes with each other. It is important to consider that relationships that have problems can often be straightened out with good boundaries between the partners and demands for mutual respect. People can forgive each other for past hurts and improve their relationship. Sometimes, this works out, but sometimes it doesn't and people need to move on to other relationships.

Sometimes, the situation is more difficult to manage. So many of us have had experience with abuse and victimization, causing us to be wary of others. We don't need to be so wary as to run and hide, but we always need to be careful, to evaluate situations with people just like we do with physical situations, such as when crossing the street or driving a car.

If we want to be able to follow our dreams and meet our goals, we need to keep the path clear. We need to take good care of ourselves so as to avoid being unnecessarily hurt along the way. It can be a rough road, but the more we keep our way clear, the easier it becomes. If we are in unhealthy relationships, are angry, resentful, or even fearful for our safety, it makes life much more difficult for us. It is our responsibility to avoid unhealthy relationships. It's hard to avoid those that occur in our own families, but we can find ways to cope better with them and even to seek help from outside if needed. I explained that in another chapter. Sometimes, it takes a lot of courage to overcome difficulties in your own family but it opens many doors.

Your dream and your personal goals are so important to you that nothing should get in the way of your accomplishing them, even though there are always challenges for you to meet. If you can keep your goals in sight, it will be easier to reach them. Even if you lose sight of them for a while or even a very long time, you can always retrieve them and find a path again. Remember that nothing is lost in life: you learn from your experiences, both pleasant and painful, and you use your knowledge to keep moving forward.

I want to emphasize again the importance of taking care of yourself in this world. It is not selfish or self-centered; it is an essential survival skill. As you become an adult, no one will look after you if you don't look after yourself. Only you can do for yourself that most necessary task: taking care of yourself. Choose friends and associates who will allow you and even help you to meet your own needs and goals. Be wary of those that don't believe or accept your dreams. Be even more wary of those who want to use you to fulfill their dreams. By the way, when you are looking out for yourself, you don't feel the need to demand of others that they look out for you. You don't feel the need to manipulate or bully others. You are independent and you feel so much better about yourself. You are empowered to be you!

So, as you learn to truly put yourself first and meet your own needs, you also become more attractive to others; you become a better friend, one that they can count on because they recognize your honesty in dealing with them. People like and respect people who are strong and straightforward. It is a quality that always serves us well. Let's add that to the Identity Scale and see where you are as you grow through your teen and young adult years.

When you are feeling good about yourself, feeling that you're on top of the world because you are in control of your life, you are at your best. That is such an incredible feeling that I hope you can experience it little by little as you take small steps, on your path to your goals.

When we hear and listen to that voice of self-love within us, we can feel extraordinarily good about ourselves as we move through the world. When we deny ourselves that success and that pleasure, we are at risk of becoming angry and resentful, of not taking good care of ourselves and then suffering the consequences of our own poor treatment. This is very sad, indeed. However, remember, you can always turn around and start acting to care for yourself. You can always listen to the voice of self-love and get moving in the right direction again.

Chapter 10

Kick Obstacles Out of Your Way: Maintain Your Momentum

In the last chapter, I talked about being careful not to let anyone get in the way of your goals, your path to your dream. I want to be clear again that some people have grand dreams such as being a professional ballplayer or a star in entertainment. Some people want to have professions where they will make a reputation for themselves as a leading professional. That is great, but dreams do not have to be grand at all. People have all kinds of dreams in all kinds of "sizes." The second decade of life is long; teens and young adults can explore different possibilities for themselves. This often goes on into the early adult years. It is actually very healthy, as there is a better chance for the dream to be a really good fit, then.

Someone can dream of managing a gas station where he works part-time now. That is a wonderful dream. Another can dream of getting married and being a homemaker. That's another wonderful dream. Or another dream can be to join the Armed Forces and make a career there. Others might dream of having jobs where they can make a decent living, but may not know or care yet what they do as long as they have enough money to be independent. All these dreams are very valuable.

The main thing about your dream is that it should fit you, not someone else. Sometimes young people follow dreams that others (usually parents or relatives) want for them: this can work well if they can adopt it as their own dream, but it won't work if they resent being told to follow a dream that doesn't meet their needs. In this chapter, I will assume that you have a dream that fits you and that you are passionate about it.

The most important thing is to get fear out of the way. We may all have doubts; that is normal. But let's be careful to avoid listening to those who say you can't do it, that you're not good enough, and that it's impossible or unrealistic. These arguments may come from other people or it may be a voice inside your head. Maybe someone has told you that in the past, and it kind of stuck in your head. It is very important to hear and then bypass that negative voice and find your own voice that knows what you want for yourself.

 Maria's Story: Maria's dream was to go to college and even to medical school to become a doctor. She was 16 years old when I saw her because she was very depressed. She lived with her mother and three younger brothers that she was responsible for after school. Her mother worked two jobs to support the family and was absent from their home until late in the evening.

Maria was depressed because she could not keep up with her homework when she had to take care of her brothers. How could she ever achieve her dreams if she could not keep up in 10th grade? Her situation is not very different from many other teens', particularly girls. It is often expected for girls to put aside their needs and help out with family situations.

How to help Maria with her situation? We tried to examine her choices. What could she do to assure time for homework? Was her mother aware of her ambition? Could she help? Could Maria do some of her homework at school? After school? Could she go to school staff to get help? Were there any relatives who could help?

Maria talked to her mother about her dreams and her mother was surprised and excited about them. She wanted her daughter to succeed even though she didn't feel all that hopeful that Maria could really accomplish all that. How could they ever afford it? But she was devoted to her family. She asked a neighbor to come over for two hours, twice a week, and watch the younger children while Maria did her schoolwork. In exchange, Maria would clean her house over the weekend when her mother was home to watch the younger children.

This would be challenging for Maria but she accepted it with enthusiasm: her dream now had a chance to become real one day. Maria's mood improved now that she had helped herself, and she found the energy to do her homework in the short time and the house cleaning she had committed to. With that, she felt she was contributing to the household and following her dreams at the same time. We call what she felt, "feeling empowered," in charge of herself and her life—the most important feeling that we can enjoy as we guide ourselves through life.

Remember that I talked about that inner voice that can be like your good, kind parent, the voice that encourages you to be you and get what you want in life, or the voice you hear from God who has a purpose for your life. This is the voice that gives you strength to go for the prize and that guides you through the challenges on your way. This is the voice that won't let you give up if you listen to it.

Gather up your courage to move ahead. It takes courage to succeed, to strive toward your goal. Don't forget that you have time. You have ten years or more to get through adolescence, identify goals, try them on, and choose one that fits your desires for yourself. Then you have the rest of your life to make it happen, or to revise it and change it as you grow. It's not a short project: you must keep at it, step by step.

Delays happen all the time. They say that "life is what happens while you are making plans." This means that all sorts of things happen that are out of your control. They do get in the way. They may slow you down, maybe even stop you in your tracks for a while. But that's OK. You will need patience (taking your time) as well as perseverance (keeping at it). When people come to see me in therapy, the first thing we talk about is patience. It will take a while for them to get out of their difficulties and get their life back on track.

Don't forget that you can almost always catch up: be creative, find different paths toward your goals. The more flexible we are, the more willing to adapt we are, the easier our path. Then, we can go with the flow and still find a way to forge ahead. Remember that the answers always lie within us and we have to find them. No one is going to do that work for us. But if we listen to our inner voice that always knows our needs, we can find at least one path toward our goal. Even if we have been much delayed, we can always get back on track. Sometimes, we need to adjust our dream and our goals, but then they become our new goals and dreams. It is also certainly OK if our goals change over time.

Sometimes, finding your path again means you have to confront those that are getting in the way. They do not have any right to block you. Getting away from anyone who is harming you or may harm you by getting in your way is very important. Remember: no one has the right to hijack your life and your dreams. They are yours and you're entitled to them even if you sometimes have to fight others for them.

Sometimes, you are tempted to go along with others even if it isn't to your advantage, because it may be easier or you need their approval. You may feel that their love is dependent on your doing their bidding. Maybe it is. But are those the persons you want to be with? This is a great challenge that we all encounter sometimes. It is tempting to just go along, but we need to choose what is more important to us: to follow our own path and be satisfied with ourselves, or to "sell out" our dreams and adjust to someone else's. Often, when you were a child, you had no choice but to go along with the others who ruled your life. But now, you are growing into your own person. For adults, it is almost always a mistake to go along with others and forsake their own needs and dreams; they then end up unhappy, resentful, and depressed.

If others really care about you, they will endorse your dreams, they will honor and respect your direction without feeling threatened in theirs. If you can resist going along, they will often prize you more and do what it takes to remain your friend or romantic partner. Being unafraid to trust yourself is the magic that makes it possible to strive for dreams and succeed in achieving them.

Finally, when you put your needs first, as you must if you are going to be a happy person, you can also be kind, generous and happy with others in your life.

Chapter 11

Coping with Problems in Your Life, Your Family, Your Community.

I have already written much about what to do when there are obstacles in your way, but there are some problems that are just so large that they need a separate chapter. Unfortunately, some of those problems are very common. Many teens have to cope with problems that interfere with their personal growth and their school achievement.

<u>Economic challenges:</u> The most common problem that affects young people, their families, and even their communities is poverty. It is the biggest handicap for parents; it often gets in the way of their functioning well, having a reasonable level of education, and being able to guide their children toward a productive life. Homes are often too small and there is sometimes a lot of instability.

Adults and children don't have space that they can call their own. They don't have the privacy to do the personal work of becoming aware of themselves and learning to manage their lives. Sometimes income is too unstable and there is homelessness for a while. This is even more challenging and destabilizing. Poor families often live on welfare and members, seeing no way out of poverty, make little effort to improve their lives. For children, living in those conditions then becomes the single biggest obstacle to being prepared for school and doing well.

Fortunately, there are public schools and there are many programs that help alleviate hunger for children and provide needed supplies. There is no shame in taking advantage of these programs: they are your due. A nationwide service, Project Head Start, has been helping families in poor neighborhoods get their young children ready for school; it has been very successful. These programs are there to help level the playing field so that everyone has a chance at a better present and a good future. Don't forget that education is due to all students and that you are entitled to seek success and follow your dreams.

The best way to get out of poverty and its overwhelming challenges, is to do whatever you can to stay in school and prepare to earn an income that will lift you out of poverty. You read in previous chapters that there is help everywhere. There are opportunities for everyone but you have to go looking for them. So, don't hesitate to go looking for opportunities for yourself. I want to remind you that there are after-school and community programs. There are public libraries where you can use computers, go online to Khan Academy and other programs to help students. With perseverance (sticking to it) and resourcefulness (get help needed), you can find the help you need.

You are entitled to a piece of the pie! You are entitled to find your success and make yourself a good life. You can even be a guide to others, helping them to find their own success.

 I'm thinking about my own history as I write this. My family lived in a tenement for the first years of my life. We received public assistance, which really helped. Still, it was very hard for my father to find work and he was often absent, seeking work somewhere else. Things became easier when I was a young teen as my father had steady work, but he became unemployed again when the business he worked for went bankrupt. Then came tough years. There was not enough food, we could not have new clothes or shoes. I remember wearing my mother's old shoes and feeling embarrassed to show up at school. But I went anyway: running away for never an option. I was brought up to face problems head-on and keep going. I thank my parents for this gift every day. You can teach yourself the same thing: it is the most valuable lesson you can learn.

After we came to the U.S., things got better. My parents could get jobs. I described earlier how both my parents worked so my sister and I could go to college full-time (a free city college), working only small jobs to pay for books and school lunches. But this was the ticket out of poverty!

Sometimes, as I wrote earlier, it takes more than one generation. We pave the way for our children to succeed. This is the story of many, many families. You can make it your story, too!

Educational challenges: At the individual level, common handicaps that get in the way of doing well in school are Attention Deficit Hyperactivity Disorder, Dyslexia, and Learning Disabilities. They are often slow to be discovered and, by that time, the students have already fallen behind and become discouraged by failure despite their best efforts to keep up. Even if you suffer from these difficulties, it is important to remember that you can catch up and have dreams just like everyone else.

Help is available at school and everyone is entitled to it. It is not embarrassing; this help is offered so that everyone has a decent chance at success. Again, help is due you and it is entirely up to you to profit from it. It is your responsibility to take full advantage of it and make your way toward your dreams.

These problems make success more challenging, but they certainly don't keep anyone from succeeding if they really want to succeed. Some people with ADHD have gone on to become doctors, one of the hardest careers. People with learning disabilities learn to meet challenges head-on and realize that they can succeed. Students with dyslexia can be very good students even if it takes them longer to read. Don't forget that these handicaps have nothing to do with intelligence; smart people are just as likely to suffer from them. Don't forget Justin Timberlake and Will Smith who are pursuing great careers while coping with their challenges.

<u>Emotional challenges</u>: difficulties such as depression and anxiety make life very difficult for those who experience them. All the advice in this book is geared toward preventing such difficulties by engaging teens and young adults to pay attention to their choices and behaviors; by fostering hope and providing tools so that they can take charge of their life, identify goals and dreams, and prosper despite difficult challenges.

But advice and encouragement are not always enough to foster well-being. Emotional pain is very hard to live with and teens and young adults sometimes get involved with drugs or engage in self-harming behaviors to lessen their pain.

Teens and young adults often seek to hide these negative behaviors due to fear or shame; however, it is most important to let the adults around you know of your emotional distress. Know that when you are in pain, it's time to get professional help, let school and college counselors know that you have difficulties. Let your parents and others who can help know that you need help. Don't forget that it is your responsibility to let your needs be known, to get the help you need to make your life the best it can be.

<u>Physical challenges</u>. Physical disabilities are challenging. However, school districts are equipped to help students with their limitations. In addition, the ADA (Americans with Disabilities Act) insures the availability of services for adults so that they can be on par with others. Physical handicaps are like other challenges: opportunities for resilience and invention. Think of that most famous physicist, Stephen Hawking, who can barely move a finger but finds ways to

share his incredible knowledge. Movie actors, Christopher Reeves and Michael J. Fox, have accomplished great things despite, or maybe because of, their injuries and illness. We see pictures of successful Special Olympic athletes everywhere. Do you know about the Reality TV show, "Little People, Big World," where the Roloff family capitalized on its members' dwarfism and showed that they are seeking success just like everyone else!

But, again, you don't have to be famous to succeed. Think back of my blind fellow student or my friend who had lost a leg in an accident. They made themselves great lives. Don't forget that, like in all things, it is up to you to know your needs and to get the help needed. Like everyone else, you can strive to meet goals, to entertain a dream, and to make your life as good as it can be.

<u>Mental/cognitive challenges</u>. Mental challenges cause individuals to have what seems to many people limited lives. However, they need to be considered like all others, with human dreams and aspirations. All people need to be included and treated without prejudice and necessary resources need to be made available.

It's most important to realize that, just like everyone else, mentally challenged persons can find purpose, satisfaction, and happiness. There are currently several coffee shops in the US that hire mentally and physically challenged staff: in a recent online post's photos, the employees in one such shop all look busy, enjoying their work, and their popularity with the customers. This is certainly good progress in acknowledging that all people need a chance to find their place in the world.

Immigrant challenges: Other students have the challenge that I had. English is not their native language: they have to learn it and then catch up with everyone else. It can be done. Many students do it and are soon at the same level as the others. They do have one advantage: they, too, have learned to work hard for what they want. This is the *real* gift of having a challenge that gets in your way: you learn the invaluable lesson of keeping at it till you succeed.

Sadly, there is right now a drive to deport persons who entered this county illegally and to refuse others trying to immigrate. This is very sad and frightening and it is very hard for the families at risk. But don't lose hope: many brave Americans are trying to help and things will change again for the better. The important thing, here, is to keep up your hope, entertain your dreams, and do what you can to bring them about. There have always been difficult times and they always came to an end. Be resilient and stay hopeful if you and your family fear or even experience deportation.

Unstable home situation: Another kind of challenge that can really get in your way and slow you down is an unstable home life. Swimming in a smooth lake is very different from swimming in rough seas. In the first one, you just need to know how to swim; in the other, you are in danger of drowning even if you are a strong swimmer. This is maybe an unusual comparison but it can certainly feel like that when your home is in turmoil.

Many teens experience unstable situations at home, at least some of the time. This can come from a lot of anger and agitation in the home, from important people in their lives coming and going, for whatever reason, from situations of separation and divorce, or even from abandonment where one parent just leaves. Many teens have parents who are divorced and they go back and forth between parents, with grandparents and others sometimes involved as well.

Sometimes, there is illness in the home, which creates a lot of stress. Alcohol and drug abuse, or sometimes illegal activities such as drug dealing, also create a lot of chaos for those engaging in this and the people living with them. As stated earlier, poverty is also very difficult to live with when there is a lack of food and other essentials, such as clothing and school supplies. It is always very difficult for children to live in such situations and they find themselves handicapped in their school work, in their making stable friendships, in managing from day to day, even.

Children and teens can find themselves so preoccupied by the home situation that they are unable to focus on themselves, on their school work, and on their dreams. If this sounds like your situation, you must understand that you really can't do anything to help your parents. That is not your job. Your job is to help yourself, to attend to your needs as much as possible and to move toward your own goals and dreams. Most important, you need to realize that this is the best thing you can do for your family now. When you are older, you may then be able to help them if you choose.

Many teens need extra help and support to get through their difficult lives, and they are more likely to get it if they seek it from the school and the community. It is your responsibility to attend to your needs as much as possible. Talk to teachers, to counselors, to helpers in community centers, to clergy in your community. Talk to your parents about getting you the help you need; they'll find it easier to support you through your challenges once you have found where to get help.

The Communities in Schools Program that I mentioned earlier seeks to assist and guide the students they care for. That program operates in the entire school as well as with individual students. With the youths' cooperation and efforts, it has been quite effective in helping them succeed. I wrote "cooperation and efforts" because it is still up to the students to make healthy choices to improve their lives.

<u>Drug and Alcohol Use:</u> Sometimes, teens living with stressful situations at home become depressed, with no hope for their future. They then take refuge in using drugs or alcohol to ease the pain of their stress and depression. This does take the pain away for a short time and may seem like an answer. But it is also a dead end. It is dangerous and it leads nowhere. So, if you are using drugs, maybe even just smoking marijuana, you are putting things in the way of getting to your goals, of making your dreams a reality. Remember that marijuana may seem helpful, but it is still illegal (in most states) and getting in trouble with the law will only hurt you.

It is certainly important to get out of that bind if you want to have a good life, a future, dreams and goals. Don't deny yourself dreams and goals. You can have those, just like everyone else. You can reach for them and get past your very difficult situation. There is help to get out of using drugs. Get the help that you need to take care of yourself, to move forward in your life. I know many people who dove into drugs but have also been able to come out of that hole and make a good life for themselves.

I know I told you that I wouldn't judge and make choices for you. However, if I can help you make better plans for yourself, I want to encourage you to do what you can to get out of using drugs before they kill you. I do have the prejudice of wanting to see you succeed. Don't blame yourself for the past, for decisions you made before you decided to take better care of yourself. Just take better care of yourself now. Listen to your voice that wants you to live a good and healthy life.

Once you get back to taking care of yourself, to loving yourself and making yourself number one, you will see that life can be very different, even if things haven't changed for your family. You can be the difference in your life. That's the secret that people who have overcome big odds know: *they can be the change that they need* and they can succeed. They can have dreams to reach for and follow. Often, they are successful if they keep at it till they succeed. An old friend once told me "you haven't failed until you stop trying."

That very wise saying means that as long as you keep trying to reach your goal, you can succeed. Remember the part where I told you that sometimes it takes a couple of generations. This means that immigrants knew that they were establishing a strong base for their children to succeed. They worked hard and their children then went to college and were successful in their careers. Actually, today it is easier for the parents to go to college too and enjoy more success.

There are all kinds of opportunities and they are yours if you just reach for them. When you play video games, you know to watch for opportunities, for special tools that you can use. You know those can help you win the game. However, if you don't pay attention, you don't really see them. This is just a game, of course, but it is a lot like life. There are a lot of things out there that are useful, but you need to pay attention to take advantage of them.

So, life is a lot like that. If you pay attention and work at finding out the opportunities, they are yours and you can have a better life. The opportunities include getting extra help at school, finding out about community programs, checking on what's available online. There are scholarships for college. Every little bit can help. It doesn't have to be difficult. Take the time to find what you need. The more goodies you have in your bag, the easier your life can be. Don't hesitate to have dreams and go after them with all your strength.

Legal involvement: In this chapter, I have been focusing on the very difficult problems that children, teens, and even young adults, often deal with in their homes. Another problem that slows young people down is having experience with the law. Many teens have had encounters with the law; they have been arrested, been held in juvenile detention, sometimes even in juvenile jail for offenses. These range from acting out and disturbing the peace, truancy from school or violating curfews, to possessing or selling drugs, theft, robbery, sometimes even possession of a weapon and assault. Even if they have not done those things themselves, many teens and young adults often know of or witness such events among their peers.

Certainly, if you have been arrested or just know others who have, you know how horrible it can be. It is a very unpleasant and scary experience. But beyond that, it is even scarier to have that on your record for all to see and know. It is true that many teens have their records sealed as they turn 18, but more and more, teens are tried as adults and those records stick with you for the rest of your life. It is surprisingly easy to get a felony record even if you think what you did was not that big a crime. Those records can make your life very difficult in terms of relationships, employment, and career opportunities. Having a legal record creates true and long-lasting obstacles to your fulfilling your dreams.

For this reason, it is very important to avoid behaviors that get you in trouble with the law. This is one of the most important things. You may think "it's just a little 'weed,'" but bad luck and an arrest will cost you a lot, maybe even get in the way of your dreams for your future. You can tell yourself that you won't be that unlucky, but you all know people who were unlucky and got locked up with charges that are now part of their record.

Many times, young adults decide to "party" once they reach legal age: now they can be "adults." This is very dangerous age as young adults put themselves at risk for poor or even very poor consequences, if they fail to take care of themselves wisely and engage in dangerous or illegal activities or behaviors. Every day brings news of teens and young adults drinking and causing horrible car accidents, where people are either killed or grievously injured.

So, the best way to take care of yourself is to listen to that inner voice that wants the best for you and to steer clear of behaviors that can get you into trouble. It is important to remember the importance of picking the right friends who will be good for you, respect your needs, and not pressure you into things you don't want to do, just because they need someone to do it with. Or worse, sometimes they need a guinea pig to experiment with; worst of all, they want a fall guy who will take the fall if they're caught doing illegal things. You may be left holding the bag.

Don't become a victim. Some people will try to use you and it is up to you to be wise and protect yourself. I know I once trusted a "so-called" friend who used me to protect himself from getting caught breaking a college rule, and got me in trouble. I was so ashamed and angry to have been used like that. Unfortunately, too many people, young and old, are eager to use others, regardless of the consequences to them. Many times, you can be charged with a crime by just being near someone who is breaking the law. Be cautious. Take care of yourself. Listen to your healthy inner voice that can tell you when you are being used or careless with your safety. I didn't listen to my voice that was telling me that my "friend" was up to no good, even though I suspected it. I have since then learned to listen to my gut-feeling and my voice got louder.

Listen to that voice that knows your dream, your intention of making yourself a good life, even if many around you act in careless or desperate ways. Some young people have become discouraged and don't even try to go for their dreams. I am hoping to wake them up and inspire them to get back on their path. They can. You can too if you have gone astray, fallen off the path to your goals. Remember that you haven't failed till you've given up.

If you do get arrested and spend time in jail or prison, it is important to still take care of yourself, to engage in any program that is offered to help you move forward. You may get counseling to help you work out your problems. It can be some sort of training to help you find jobs after you get out. Don't give up on your life just because you have challenges now. You know that you can make your life better if you embrace the better path; I hope you will try as hard as you can. You will get out earlier and you will do better after leaving jail if you have prepared for your life back in the world. There are programs to help you get back on track and find your dreams and goals again.

Building Your Best Life

So, there are major problems in your life -- they can be the assets that propel you forward to success. Don't be afraid to have big dreams. It is important not to "shrink" them because you don't believe you can accomplish them. You won't know until you try. Many people succeed despite or maybe because of the challenge of their difficulties. They have that special gift: being able to face and overcome challenges. No one can take that away from them. They often become leaders who show others the way, or helpers who help others meet their challenges. Gather up your courage, keep your dreams in sight! You can be that person!

Many people who succeed do so because they've learned to over-come the odds that were stacked against them. They refused to give up and stood up to the challenges. This instinct is built-in, just like the toddler who wants to walk and keeps trying until he gets it right despite all the falls and frustrations. Toddlers don't even view it as frustrations: they are so determined to do it that all their energy goes toward their goal.

The earlier in life you learn to overcome problems, the more likely you are to succeed. Remember the people who had not encountered problems before college had a harder time than those who had al-ready learned to manage obstacles and challenges. Just like when you are exposed to a disease, your body builds antibodies to fight off the invader; when you are challenged, you gather your resources to man-age the challenge. Antibodies stay in your body your whole life; so, do the courage and strength you develop when overcoming challenges.

Young people who face challenges can learn to be more resilient. This is particularly true if they can find support at home, at school, or in the community. But the most important support is the one you have within you.

 I remember coming across a picture of a bird sitting on a tiny branch in a bush. The caption said that it wasn't worried because it wasn't relying on the branch to hold it up, but on its own power to fly. That is one of the most important lessons in life. You will fly by your own strength, and by your strength alone, not on the support you get, or even lack.

So, whether it is because of a very difficult life imposed on you and/or mistakes that you have made, don't give up on yourself. That is the worst mistake you can make. Hang on to your hopes and dreams for yourself, and listen to your inner voice that will guide you towards a better life. Everyone is entitled to a good life, even you. No one is so "bad" that they have to forswear a good life. Be courageous. It takes true courage to get out of difficulties and make a good life for yourself.

Conclusion

In these many chapters I have outlined and then explained the many lessons that you need to learn to make your life as good as possible. These chapters are meant to help you on your path through the teen years and beyond. They have shown you that there is a lot to do and have reminded you that you have time, plenty of time (ten years and more) to find your way through your second decade and onto your early adult years.

You have learned how to use the Identity Scale and the Behavior Scale to help you find direction and appreciate your efforts. You have learned to use Decision Trees to see into the future, to see consequences to your actions/choices, and to help you make choices that fit you best. You have learned the many lessons about how to take care of yourself, grow your dreams, and create your own path as you learn to manage your life and make it what you want.

My hope is that you have found these chapters useful and helpful and that you are enjoying your path to your future. I hope that you are feeling challenged and hopeful. I hope that you understand that there are many exciting paths to your future and that they are all right; the only wrong one is to give up on your future.

a tree's whisper

how do i be me? she asked the tree
and she heard its whisper -
listen to the beat of your heart,
stand tall in your roots,
stretch your arms to the sky
as you claim your presence.
and you'll know there's nothing else
for you to do but to be you.
© Terri St. Cloud

Reprinted here by permission of the author

Appendix

The Behavior and Identity Scales and a blank Decision Tree
are available for download at www.iwanttobeme.org
Please use Code: bisdt2017

Instructions for the Identity Scale

Since the opening chapters of this book, I have been mentioning the Identity Scale. It was the centerpiece, the most important part of the original workshop, and it is one of the most important parts of the book. It is like a mirror. This is where you will see and understand not only where you are now but where you want to be, what your goals are.

Earlier in the book, I wrote that your identity is the way you describe yourself, the way you and others see you. You know your physical characteristics, your age, gender, height, weight, hair, and eye color. You know your ethnicity, your heritage. This last is complicated for most of us.

Describing qualities that are not physical is more difficult. You know them and they do "show" when others get to know you but it's not so easy to be aware of them and able to name them. However, it is most important to be aware of them and able to identify them by name. Why? Because, it is only when you are aware of who you are that you can make the choices that fit you. You will see what I mean very shortly.

This is your Identity Scale. It is private. Only you can see it. Only you can make changes to it. Of course, you can show it to others if you like, but it is your private scale to do with as you wish.

The Identity Scale has many pairs of opposite qualities. Most are rather general and it is up to you to decide how they fit you or rather how you fit on the scale. For each pair, there will be three measurements.

The first marker, P for Past, is to evaluate where you were before you became a teen. Think of yourself before this period and decide where you were on the scale. This is entirely up to you where you place your P; it is entirely your private experience.

Next is T. T is for Today and you can decide where you are every time you check out the Identity Scale. It is important. Was there some movement for you? In which direction? Maybe no movement? Is that what you want?

The last marker, F for Future is also very important. Place it where you would like to be. This way, you can see what you are wishing for yourself, what you are working toward. This button can move as you go along: you may set different goals for yourself.

When I did this exercise with teens, they were immediately excited. Being able to have this glimpse at themselves really spoke to them. I hope it is useful for you, too.

Think of the book's cover. It shows a teen searching for who she is, trying to find her direction. This scale is to help you see more clearly who you are and where you are going.

Some terms are easy to understand; others need explanation. Teens who are ambitious have goals that they want to reach. Discouraged teens have given up on goals for themselves. Excitable teens get angry easily. They have a bad temper. Teens who are independent do things by themselves and make their own decisions. Dependent teens need others to tell them what to do. Jealous teens think others have it better. Secure teens look at themselves and decide what they want for themselves.

I have also left blank spaces for you to add your own pairs of qualities that are important or difficult for you.

The position of each marker will change only if you change it. I do encourage you to change the Today marker as often as you need to show a change. You may also want to change the Future marker as needed. You may even change the Past marker if you remember something different and want to change it.

Identity Scale

Happy..Sad

Outgoing...Shy

Friendly...Unfriendly

Hopeful...Hopeless

Ambitious...Discouraged

Relaxed...Worried

Bad temper..Cool

Peaceful..Angry

Independent...Dependent

Brave...Fearful

Secure..Insecure

Jealous..Not jealous

Kind...Mean

Loving..Hating

Truthful..Lying

Respectful....................................Manipulative

Focused..Scattered

Confident......................................Insecure

Active...Slow-moving

Honest..Cheating

Caring...Careless

Trusting..Scared

Courageous...................................Discouraged

Straightforward ....Devious

....

....

....

....

....

Instructions for the Behavior Scale

In the original workshop, there was only the Identity Scale. In this book, I have added the Behavior Scale to help you appraise the choices you make, the behaviors you engage in.

Your choice of behavior is very important for your present and for the future you are creating. It is essential to think about these choices and be honest with yourself when using the scale. Remember that no one else will see this. It is your private place. I hope that holding this mirror up to yourself will help you see more clearly where you are and, most important, where you want to be. You can get there. The more honest you are, the easier it will be for you as you will be forging a straight path to your goals.

Here again, you will have the three markers, P for Past, T for Today, and F for Future, that you can use to see where you have been, where you are now, and where you want to be. Most important is to move these markers often to show any change in your direction. Are you going in the direction that you want?

Finally, you have blank spaces to add behaviors that are important or challenging for you.

Behavior Scale

Eating breakfast	No breakfast
Doing homework	No homework
Obeying parents	Disobeying parents
Doing classwork	no classwork
Being calm in class	Acting out in class
Obeying teachers	Disobeying teachers
Managing school behavior	Getting detention/suspended
Attending school	Skipping school
Obeying the law	Having legal troubles
Being honest	Cheating, Lying/Stealing
Studying for tests	Blowing off tests
Treating others well	Bullying others
Eating regular meals	Skipping meals
Helping at home	Refusing responsibility

Helping brothers and sisters..Avoiding caring

Personal cleanliness...Poor personal care

Being careful...Engaging in risky behaviors

Being independent..Joining a gang

Being respectful...Mocking others

Being sober...Drinking alcohol

Being drug free...Using drugs

No tobacco...Smoking tobacco

No pot..Smoking pot

Steering clear..Selling drugs/pot

....

....

....

....

Learning to Use Decision Trees

First, let me say that they are not as difficult as they look. When you look at the blank decision tree on the next page, it looks very complicated. But, let's look carefully. We start at the first box on the left: the decision to be made. It's a YES/NO choice. You decide YES, then consider what happens next, again a YES/NO result and new choice. Or you decide NO, then consider what happens next, again a YES/NO result and new choice. This just keeps going.

The challenge is to take one step at a time. Keep the goal in mind but do not jump to the goal or conclusion. The outcome of the goal is always in the last column on the right. We are trying to see how decisions may or may not lead to the desired goal. Learning to look at choices STEP by STEP is the lesson.

1. So, let's look at a simple one. **Luis's goal is to do well in Math**. The problem is that he has Math class right before lunch and he is often too hungry to pay attention. Math is really hard and if he is hungry and distracted, it becomes impossible to listen and participate in class, just total frustration. Luis has been told that he should have breakfast to avoid this problem. He never has breakfast and doesn't really believe that having breakfast will make a difference. However, Luis is willing to try it out and experiment with different breakfasts.

2. So, the first question in the box on the left is **Whether to have breakfast?** The next column answers that question with NO and YES. Let's follow the NO branch. The next

question is **Hungry?** The next column answers that question with NO and YES. Let's follow the NO branch first. Luis is not hungry. The question is **Paying Attention?** The next column answers that question with NO and YES.

3. Then we go back to the second column that asked **Hungry?** The next column answers that question with NO and YES. Let's follow the YES branch this time. He is uncomfortable, **paying attention?** Again, we move next to the NO and YES boxes. NO says **Not paying attention.** YES states that he is **paying attention.** Maybe Luis has very good self-control and can pay attention even if he is very hungry. The next step is to go back to Column 1, **Having Breakfast?** and then follow the YES answer. So, the next question is **Healthy, nutritious breakfast?** The next column answers that question with NO and YES. Let's follow the NO branch first. Let's again take the NO branch first since it is on top. Luis eats junk food. The question is **Hungry?** The next column answers that question with NO and YES. The last question is **paying attention?** The next column again answers that question with NO and YES.

4. You can see that by looking at each step, you can make out what is likely to happen depending on your choices. Alternately, if Luis does experiment, he can record what did happen, whether he had breakfast or not.

Next, let's make a decision tree for **Sha'anice who had to decide between going to a forbidden party and studying.** If she decided to go to the party, she'd have to lie to her mother about studying with a friend. She knew that no one would be supervising the party. It was a secret. The party could be fun, but there might also be pot and beer present. Things could possibly get out of hand. A neighbor might call the police if the kids were rowdy. She might drink and smoke, risk her personal safety and engage in sex with a random partner.

Of course, you might say that she won't know this till after the party has happened, but the truth is that she (and you) can and need to think about it before hand. This way, she and you can make more knowing choices for yourselves.

Let's look at the decision tree I built for Sha'anice's decision about whether to go to the party/lie to her mother. Follow each branch from left to right, to its conclusion, just like you did with the Breakfast decision.

You can see that by looking at each step, you can make out what could happen depending on her choices. None of us knows the future but we can make good guesses and consider our path carefully. In the last box on the right, I suggest that the only way she could do well on the test if she skipped studying, went to the party, smoked and drank, is by cheating...she could not realistically do well (honestly) under those circumstances.

Remember that this is not about judging yourself, but judging your decisions – it is about looking carefully at decisions and making the ones that work best for you.

We're going to do one more. This is one is going to be for **Cameron's very difficult decision: whether to have sex with a romantic partner.** Often, your partner may want to have sex but you are not sure. Do you do it to please him or her? Are you afraid of being rejected if you don't have sex with the partner? Do you put your needs first? Do you insist on safe sex if you are having sex? What are the consequences of each decision? See if you can follow that one without it being spelled out.

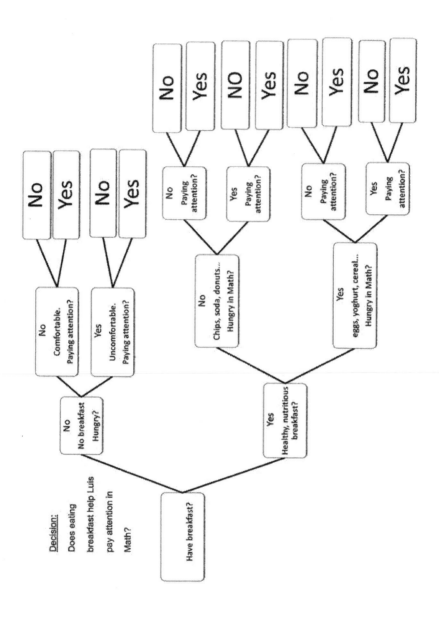

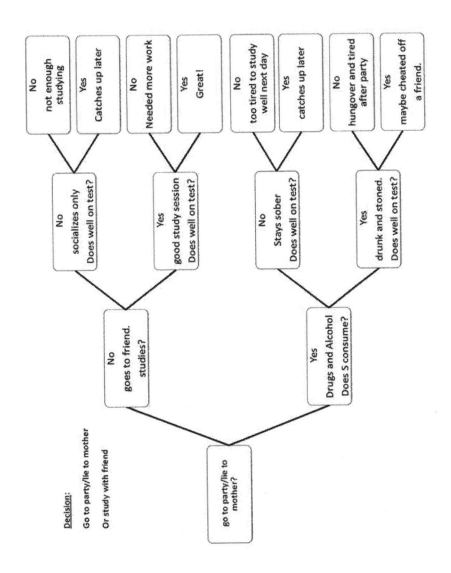

Decision:

Go to party/lie to mother

Or study with friend

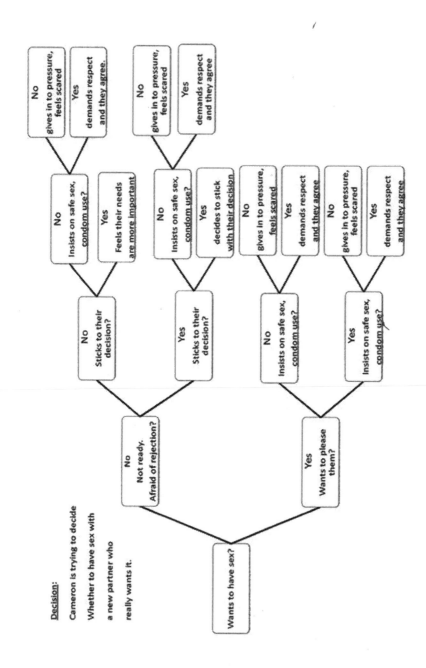

Decision:

Cameron is trying to decide
Whether to have sex with
a new partner who
really wants it.

Wants to have sex?

No
Not ready.
Afraid of rejection?

Yes
Wants to please
them?

No
Sticks to their
decision?

Yes
Sticks to their
decision?

No
Insists on safe sex,
condom use?

Yes
Insists on safe sex,
condom use?

No
Insists on safe sex,
condom use?

Yes
Feels their needs
are more important

No
Insists on safe sex,
condom use?

Yes
decides to stick
with their decision

No
gives in to pressure,
feels scared

Yes
demands respect
and they agree

No
gives in to pressure,
feels scared

Yes
demands respect
and they agree

No
gives in to pressure,
feels scared

Yes
demands respect
and they agree

No
gives in to pressure,
feels scared

Yes
demands respect
and they agree

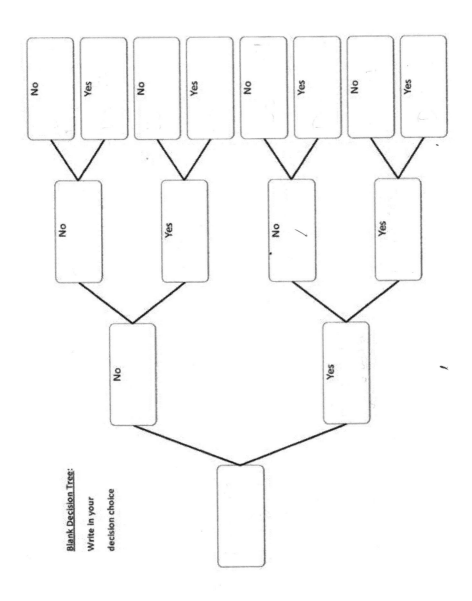

Blank Decision Tree:

Write in your

decision choice

Reading Recommendations

Books for Teens

<u>Note</u>: Most books for teens are very suitable for young adults, as well.

Canfield, Jack & Kent Healy. 2008. *The Success Principles for Teens.* How to get from where you are to where you want to be. Health Communications.

Covey, Sean. 2006. *The 6 Most Important Decisions You'll Ever Make.* A Fireside Book/Simon & Schuster.

Friel, John C. & Linda D. Friel. 2000. *The Seven Best Things Smart Teens Do.* Health Communications.

Graham, Stedman. 2000. *Teens Can Make It Happen.* Nine Steps to Success. A Fireside Book/Simon & Schuster.

Graham, Stedman. 2001. *Teens Can make It Happen Workbook.* A Fireside Book/Simon & Schuster.

Healy, Kent & Kyle Healy. 2005. *Cool Stuff They Should Teach You in School*. Cool Stuff Media.

Leslie, Roger. 2004. *Success Express for Teens*. 50 Activities that will change your life. Bayou Publishing.

Marcus, David L. 2009. *Acceptance:* A Legendary Guidance Counselor Helps Seven Kids Find the Right Colleges—and Find Themselves. Penguin Press, New York.

Schab, Lisa M. 2013. *The Self-Esteem Workbook for Teens*. Activities to help you build confidence and achieve your goals. Instant Help Books/New Harbinger Publications

Book(s) for Teen Girls

Hemmen, Lucy, Ph.D. 2015. *The Teen Girl's Survival Guide:* Ten Tips for Making Friends, Avoiding Drama, and Coping with Social Stress. The Instant Help Books.

Roberts, Emily. 2015. *Express Yourself.* A teen girl's guide to speaking up and being who you are. Instant Help Books/New Harbinger Publications.

<u>Note</u>: There are several more very good books in the Instant Help Books Series.

Books for Young Adults

Angone, Paul. 2013. *Secrets for Your Twenties*. Moody Publishers.

Brown, Kelly Williams. 2013. *Adulting:* How to Become a Grown Up in 468 Easy(ish) Steps. Grand Central Publishing. Hachette Book Group.

Harper, Hill. 2006. *Letters to a Younger Brother:* MANifest Your Destiny. Gotham Books.

Hawkins, John. 2017. *101 Things All Young Adults Should Know*. River Grove Books.

McGraw, Jay. 2000. *Life Strategies for Teens*. Fireside.

Poodiak, Kathy, PA-C. 2017. *Being Your Best Self; A Young Adult's Guide to Conscious Living*. Mazo Publishers.

Siegel, Cary. 2016. *Why Didn't They Teach Me This in School?* 99 Personal Money Management Principles to Live By. Simple Strategic Solutions, LLC.

Books for Parents

Damour, Lisa, PhD. 2016. *Untangled*. Guiding teenage girls through the seven transitions into adulthood. Ballantine Books.

Dyer, Wayne W. 2010. *What Do You Really Want for Your Children?* HarperCollins e-books,

Faber, Elaine & Elaine Mazlich. 1999. *How to talk so teens will listen and listen so teens will talk.* Collins.

McRae, Barbara, MCC. 2004. *Coach Your Teen to Success.* 7 Simple steps to transform relationships and enrich lives. Book Baby.

Marcus, David L. 2009. *Acceptance:* A Legendary Guidance Counselor Helps Seven Kids Find the Right Colleges—and Find Themselves. Penguin Press, New York.

O'Grady, Colleen. 2015. *Dial Down the Drama:* Reducing Conflict and Reconnecting with Your Teenage Daughter--A Guide for Mothers Everywhere. Amacom.

Orenstein, Peggy. 2016. *Girls and Sex.* Navigating the complicated new landscape. Harper/Harper Collins Publishers.

Sales, Nancy Jo. 2016. *American Girls.* Social media and the secret lives of teenagers. Alfred A. Knopf.

Siegel, Daniel J. MD. 2013. *Brainstorm.* The Power and Purpose of the Teenage Brain. An inside-out guide to the emerging adolescent mind, ages 12-24. Jeremy P. Tarcher/Penguin.

Wolf, Anthony, E. Ph.D. 1991, 2002. *Get Out of My Life, but First Could You Drive Me and Cheryl to the Mall?* A parent's guide to the new teenager. Farrar, Straus, and Giroux.

Two More Great Books

Doty, James, MD. 2016. *Into the Magic Shop*: A Neurosurgeon's Quest to Discover the Mysteries of the Brain and the Secrets of the Heart. Avery/Penguin Random House.

Quin, Daniel. 1992. *Ishmael*: A Novel. Bantam Books/Random House/Penguin Random House.

Acknowledgements

This work had been on my mind for two decades but I didn't know what shape it would take. It then became a guidebook thanks to Bill O'Hanlon who has also inspired many others to get their project in writing. It has taken two years to bring it to fruition thanks to the encouragement of family members and friends. Grateful thanks go to my sister, Anne Weiss, and her husband, Robert, who mothered me on weekends when I came, totally exhausted, for respite in their home.

Many friends who inspired me to persevere are no longer on this earth but their spirit kept me moving forward. Dr. Diane Thomas gave me the opportunity to formulate the initial workshop; my dear friend, David Sale tan, PhD, taught me to never give up. Last, but not least, Francoise Dolto, MD, an eminent French psychiatrist and child psychoanalyst of the last century, who has contributed greatly to our understanding of children's identity development, brought me to the study and practice of psychology. I thank her for her tireless devotion to revealing the extent to which human beings need authenticity and truth to develop optimally. With these conditions met, they can overcome any adversity at any age. I also owe a debt of gratitude to her daughter, Doctor Catherine Dolto, a physician and writer who has greatly contributed to the field of emotional development, and who encourages me as I follow my path as a psychologist and a writer.

Among my many friends who encouraged me, I want to thank Louie Saletan who, like his father, took me seriously and spent hours editing the first draft of this book; then, David's widow, Jeanne Saletan, carefully edited the last version! Thanks also to my devoted friend, Dorothy Robbins, who read my manuscript between rehabilitation sessions as she recovered from a bad fall. My daughter, Corinne Martch, MA, added enthusiasm and the timely examples that my generation is so far removed from. My son, Marc Sawaya, who became my creative partner, agreeing to be artist, web-designer, researcher, editor, and general technical support, provided tremendous support in moving this book to completion. I am very excited that this work has encouraged him to offer his services as a free-lance web designer, something he had been "itching" to do for some time.

Many others have contributed ideas and support for the last two years. Dr. Harriet Arvey read the entire manuscript and was very encouraging. My Master Mind group was especially helpful in keeping me accountable and on track. Dani Antman, Patricia Schwartz, and Doreen Lerner, PhD, were wonderful partners in this support group. I wish them success with their endeavors as well.

Many more have shared my enthusiasm for this work and given me encouragement on the way. Colleagues, especially, kept me on my toes with frequent inquiries as to my progress! I thank Drs. Hillery Keith and Susan Chanderbhan-Forde, suite mates, for their constant support and offers to read chapters. Dr. Allen E. Ivey provided positive feedback and encouragement with his endorsement. Sarah Fisher offered much enthusiasm for my endeavor and a Courage mug of her own design – this was used Monday mornings to dive back into the week. Joan Kosinski provided encouragement and support from afar. Another colleague, John Morris, proffered welcome support and enthusiasm at the end of the process-- just when I needed it!

Finally, I have found profound encouragement and inspiration in the ongoing work of many colleagues, some well-known in the field of human development. I have recommended their work here when it was applicable.

Thank You for Reading

Volume 1 of the *I Want To Be Me Series*!

Watch for the next volume:

A guidebook for Pre-Teens and Young Teens,

to come out within a year!

Register at http://iwanttobeme.org for announcements.

I hope this guide was helpful

and I welcome reviews on Amazon.com!

Thank You!